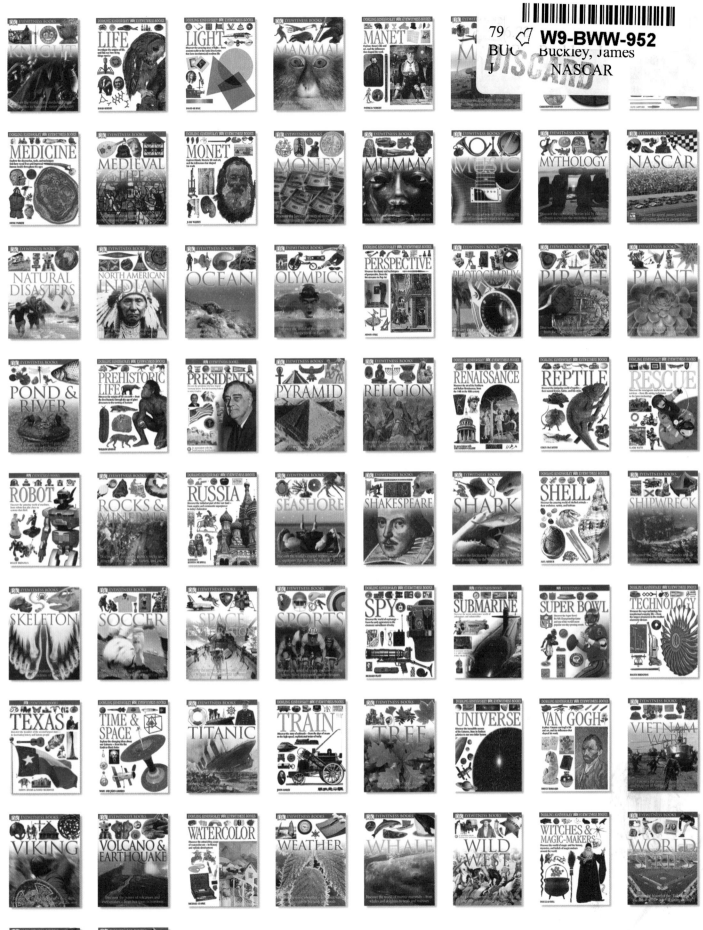

Eyewitness
NASCAR

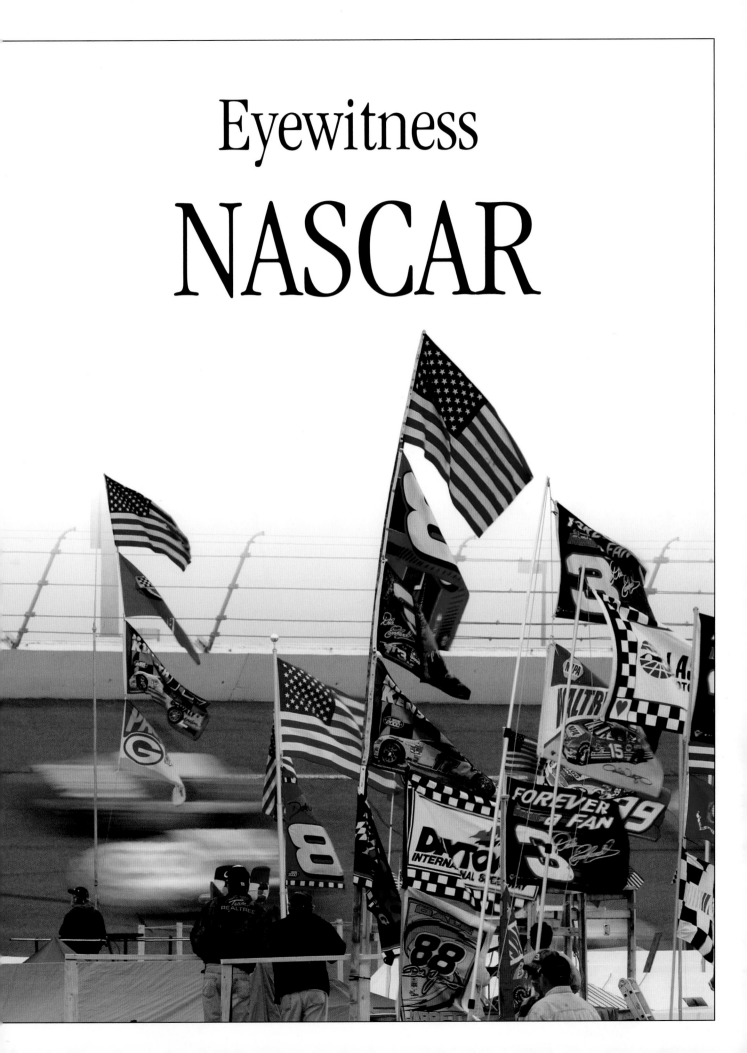

Pontiac car ad

Crew pushing car to starting grid

RICHARD PETTY
STP
GOODYEAR
UNION

Richard Petty's helmet

DAYTONA
INTERNATIONAL SPEEDWAY CORP.
DAYTONA BEACH, FLA.
500 MILE NASCAR
INTERNATIONAL
SWEEPSTAKES
NO MONEY REFUNDED
RAIN CHECK
SUNDAY
FEB'RY
22
1959
12:00 NOON

1959 Daytona 500 ticket

Gasman wearing protective apron

Official's radio

RUSTY WALLACE

Rusty Wallace bobblehead doll

NASCAR convertible race car

J.H. PETTY'S GARAGE
GREENSBORO, N.C.
BOB WELBORN
49
FRED GADDY CHEVROLET
LENOIR, N.C.
GOOD/YEAR

Eyewitness
NASCAR

Written by
JAMES BUCKLEY, JR.

DK Publishing, Inc.

Dale Earnhardt
souvenir bracelet

LONDON, NEW YORK, MUNICH,
MELBOURNE, and DELHI

Editor Elizabeth Hester
Senior Designer Tai Blanche
Assistant Managing Art Editor Michelle Baxter
Creative Director Tina Vaughan
Publishing Director Beth Sutinis
Jacket Art Director Dirk Kaufman
Production Manager Ivor Parker
DTP Coordinator Milos Orlovic
Contributing Editor Laura Buller

Produced by
Shoreline Publishing Group LLC
President/Editorial Director James Buckley, Jr.
Designer Diana Catherines, DesignDesign

NASCAR Publishing
Senior Manager of Publishing Jennifer White
Publishing Coordinator Catherine McNeill
Manager of Communications, NASCAR NEXTEL
Cup Series Herb Branham

This edition published in the United States in 2005
by DK Publishing, Inc.
375 Hudson Street, New York, NY 10014

06 07 08 09 10 9 8 7 6 5 4 3 2

Library of Congress Cataloging-in-Publication Data
Buckley, James, 1963-
   Nascar / written by James Buckley, Jr.-- 1st American ed.
      p. cm. -- (Eyewitness books)
   Includes index.
   ISBN 0-7566-1194-6 (plc) -- ISBN 0-7566-1193-8 (alb)
   1. Stock car racing--United States--Juvenile literature. 2.
NASCAR (Association)--Juvenile literature. I. Title. II.
Series: DK eyewitness books.
GV1029.9.S74B843 2005
796.72'0973--dc22
                                        2005002310

Color reproduction by Colourscan, Singapore
Printed in China by Toppan Printing Co., (Shenzhen) Ltd.

Discover more at
www.dk.com

Kurt Busch

Elliott
Sadler's
car

Racing at Daytona

Driver's
gloves

1969 Daytona 500 program

Darrell Waltrip

Contents

Curtis Turner's car

What is NASCAR?

NASCAR STANDS FOR the National Association for Stock Car Auto Racing. Founded in 1948 to give an official structure to the many races happening throughout the south, NASCAR has been growing steadily ever since. Today, there are NASCAR fans in every state and across the globe.

WELCOME SIGN
This billboard welcomes racing fans to a day at the track. There are 32 NASCAR tracks, with more planned across United States.

Millons watch the races on television, and race lovers pack the stands at tracks every weekend. The top series in NASCAR, the NASCAR NEXTEL Cup, features more than 35 high-profile races each year. More than 45 drivers take part, competing to place well and earn points toward a chance to become a NASCAR champion.

SPEED WINS!
NASCAR race cars average as much as 160 mph (257 km/h) in a race, and can reach top speeds of more than 180 mph (290 km/h). Drivers such as Casey Mears (above) thrill fans with their daring determination to finish at the front of the pack.

Helmets and fire-retardant safety gear help protect the crew.

The long neck of a fuel can funnels gas to the car's tank.

BUCKLE UP FOR SAFETY
NASCAR drivers, such as Jamie McMurray (left), strap themselves into their drivers' seats securely. Many pieces of special safety equipment, from helmets to huge seat belts, help protect drivers in case of an accident.

All four tires are usually changed at each pit stop; sometimes, though, a team may only change two.

FRIENDLY FOLKS
NASCAR drivers are among the most accessible athletes in sports. They spend many hours meeting fans, promoting the sport, and supporting sponsor and community programs. Drivers (like Jeff Gordon, above) may sign autographs right up until race time.

Each pit crew member has a specific job, such as operating an airdrill, so stops are fast and efficient.

Championship Cup

In 2004, the top series in NASCAR adopted a new points system for determining each year's champion. Drivers earn points throughout the season for finishing position, laps led, and other factors. After the first 26 races, the 10 drivers with the most points enter the "Chase for the NASCAR NEXTEL Cup" over the season's final 10 races. At the end of the season, the "Top 10" driver with the most points is the champion.

The championship trophy is inspired by the checkered flags waved at the finish line.

GREAT START
NASCAR's creation of the "Chase for the NASCAR NEXTEL Cup" in 2004 promised to add an exciting finish to the end of the regular race season.

Rank	+/-	Driver	Points	Behind	Starts	Poles	Wins	Top5	Top10	Winnings
		Dale Earnhardt, Jr.	5954	-98	33	0	5	15	15	$6,631,920

NASCAR NEXTEL Cup Series

KEEPING SCORE
Drivers get points for wins, finishing place, and laps led during a race. This sample scoring line gives an at-a-glance summary of a driver's standings.

Points by which this driver trails the points leader

Races run in current season

Each win earns 180 points.

Number of times starting from pole (first) position

Total money won from races run in current season

THE FIRST WINNER CLAIMS THE CUP
Competition for the top spot is intense. Because there are relatively few points separating the first from the tenth driver, any of the top ten drivers has a shot at winning. In 2004, Kurt Busch came out on top with 6,506 points.

FOUR BY FOUR
Unlike some other styles of car racing, NASCAR racing features two, three, or even four cars sometimes racing side by side. It's too dangerous for cars to pass this close through the curves on the track, so each straight section of the track becomes a mini-race to see who can gain the edge by entering the next curve first.

With only inches—and often less—between each car, rivers must maintain complete control.

A main sponsor logo helps identify each car—and provides advertising in return for funding for the race team.

Smaller sponsors are represented with stickers on the fender.

NASCAR MEANS TEAMWORK
NASCAR racing is about more than a great driver in a fast car. More than 100 people contribute to making each racing team a success, from the car designers to the mechanics to the pit crew (shown here) that services the car on race day.

Birth of NASCAR

Rexford's No. 60 car

THERE'S AN OLD SAYING IN RACING: the first car race was held on the day the *second* car was built. Race cars have been around since the late 1800s. Most of them were specially built to race at top speed. But in the 1930s, drivers began racing their family cars. Cars that are not modified for racing are called "stock cars," since they come directly from a car dealers' stock, or supply. By the late 1940s, stock car racing had become so popular, especially in the Southeastern states, that an organization was needed to set uniform rules. In 1948, the National Association for Stock Car Auto Racing (NASCAR) was born.

A TOAST TO THE CHAMP
This commemorative cup honors Bill Rexford, who won the 1950 NASCAR championship title with 11 top-10 finishes in 17 races.

A leather helmet provided little protection for early drivers.

France's small car was a 2-seater, unlike most cars of his era.

DRIVER TO PIONEER
The man leaning on this No. 10 Ford is the founding father of NASCAR. In 1947, "Big" Bill France, Sr. organized a meeting of drivers and others involved in stock car racing. From that meeting came the organization known as NASCAR. France, himself a driver, also helped lay out the first race course on Daytona Beach, Florida (now the home of the prestigious Daytona 500). France guided NASCAR until 1972, and died in 1992.

GULF

Steel roll bar for safety

Most early sponsors were local, not national, companies.

J.H. PETTY'S GARAGE
GREENSBORO, N.C.

BOB WELBORN

FRED GADDY CHEVROLET
LENOIR, N.C.

GOODYEAR

Eye-catching paint schemes draw attention to the sponsor's logo.

Sponsors' names cover the car.

DRIVER CURTIS TURNER

SCHWAM MOTOR CO.
CHARLOTTE, N.C.

What we say it is—it is SCHWAM

TOPS DOWN
One division of early NASCAR racing competed in convertibles such as this No. 49 Chevrolet, which was driven by Bob Welborn. The last convertible race in NASCAR was in 1959.

SPONSORS SHOW THE WAY
A key part of the successful rise of NASCAR in its early days was the support of businesses that paid money to help put cars into races. Sponsors such as Schwam Motors, on Curtis Turner's 1955 car, got to display signs on the cars in exchange for financial support.

Official number to help fans easily track their favorites

NASCAR'S TOP AWARD GOES TO PONTIAC!
Undisputed Grand National Champ Over All Stock Cars Regardless of Size-Power-Price!

92 FAB

THE POWER OF NASCAR
Car manufacturers quickly realized that having their cars do well in races would help them sell cars to fans. This 1957 ad for Pontiac cars touts the fact that the brand had won the NASCAR title (then called the Grand National) the year before. Drivers and team owners worked with car makers to help create better and more powerful cars that appealed to racers and the general public alike.

Advertisement for the brand of car: the Hudson Hornet

When the tide rolled in, the race was off—beachside racing could only be held at low-tide.

RACING ON THE BEACH AT DAYTONA

The hard, flat sand on Daytona Beach, Florida, was the site of some of the earliest stock car races. Drivers sped along a track on the beach before making this turn back onto the roadway to complete a lap. The ocean's roar competed with the sound of powerful engines as fans crowded along the edge of the track to cheer for their favorites.

DOWN AND DIRTY DRIVING

Dirt tracks, from a quarter mile to one mile (0.4 to 1.6 km) long were built in many Southern cities. Dirt-track racing was tough on the cars—and on the drivers. The rough-surfaced tracks were often rutted and bumpy. Stock cars, built for smooth roads, took a beating, particularly the tires and the suspension. With no seat belts or safety gear, drivers had a rough ride, too. Soon asphalt race tracks would replace dirt tracks.

NASCAR NEXTEL CUP CHAMPIONS	
1949	Red Byron
1950	Bill Rexford
1951	Herb Thomas
1952	Tim Flock
1953	Herb Thomas
1954	Lee Petty
1955	Tim Flock
1956	Buck Baker
1957	Buck Baker
1958	Lee Petty
1959	Lee Petty

Driver's name

Door handle—no longer a feature on stock cars

Glass windshield

KEY CAR OF THE EARLY ERA

Though no longer made today, the Hudson Hornet brand of car was one of the top winners in the early days of NASCAR. Herb Thomas won two NASCAR titles and was runner-up twice while steering this big, powerful machine.

Hood ornament

HERB THOMAS

OUS HUDSON 92

RNET

CHAMPION

NASCAR in the 1960s

NASCAR'S SECOND FULL DECADE was one of steady growth, both in attendance and prize money. New driving legends were born and new rivalries were formed. The cars themselves became more powerful and began to be built for racing only. Earlier cars were constructed from passenger cars; by 1969, they were race cars from the very start. Richard Petty won the first two of his seven career titles in this decade.

Roberts' crew chief, "Banjo" Matthews

GETTING UP TO SPEED

A star driver in the early 1960s, Glenn "Fireball" Robert (right) is shown here marveling at his qualifying speed at a 1962 race in North Carolina. In the days before radio-equipped helmets, chalkboards like this one were used by pit crews during races to communicate with the driver. This one is upside down for no particular reason.

DAYTONA BLOSSOMS

The mighty superspeedway at Daytona Beach was only a year old at this 1960 Firecracker 250 race, but it was already considered one of the finest stock-car racing track in America. Four NASCAR races were held there in 1960, with Junior Johnson winning the Daytona 500. The grandstands shown here were later enlarged to accomdate the growing crowds.

PIT CREWS HEAT UP

In the 1960s, the speed of pit crews improved tremendously. Top teams realized that a rapid pit stop could mean the difference between victory and defeat. Here, the 1962 crew of Joe Weatherly takes part in a pit-crew race, which they won by changing two tires and adding 10 gallons of gas in 27 seconds. Today's crews can finish a similar race in less than 15 seconds.

A jack is used to lift the side of the car off the ground so the tires can be changed.

Front tires turn in the direction of the skid to help the driver keep control.

A DUSTY FIREBALL

Fireball Roberts shows off some of the power of his 410-horsepower Ford during this 1963 race, as he skids off the asphalt and onto the dirt apron around the track. Note the "410 HP" displayed proudly on the hood. Cars equipped with such large engines helped speeds increase throughout the decade.

POWERING UP PROGRESS

As the prestige and prize money increased in this decade, racing teams competed to create larger and more powerful engines. NASCAR raced along with them, trying to craft rules that kept one team from having too much of an advantage over the others. The back-and-forth battle led to the solid set of rules used today.

Because they were "stock" cars that were originally passenger cars, racing cars of this era still had headlights, even though there were no night races.

A TRIO OF SIXTIES STARS

Posing before the start of the 1968 Daytona 500 are three NASCAR legends. Richard Petty (left) won two of his seven career season titles in the 1960s. This race was the first of three Daytona 500s that Cale Yarborough (center) would win in his career. And in 1969, LeeRoy Yarbrough (right) became the first driver to win NASCAR's "Triple Crown," by capturing the Daytona 500, the World 600, and the Southern 500 in one year.

SILVER FOX

Three-time NASCAR NEXTEL Cup champion David Pearson, known as the "Silver Fox," is second only to Richard Petty on the all-time race victory list. Pearson racked up 105 wins during his storied career. He was known as a patient, steady driver, but also as one who was more than willing to "trade paint," or bump against other cars, if it meant taking the lead. His son Larry became a top racer as well.

NASCAR NEXTEL CUP CHAMPIONS	
1960	Rex White
1961	Ned Jarrett
1962	Joe Weatherly
1963	Joe Weatherly
1964	Richard Petty
1965	Ned Jarrett
1966	David Pearson
1967	Richard Petty
1968	David Pearson
1969	David Pearson

NASCAR in the 1970s

THIS DECADE WAS ONE OF enormous change for stock car racing. From a small and regionally popular sport, NASCAR was beginning to blossom into a national phenomenon. For the first time, a major national sponsor signed on to sponsor the organization, increasing prize money and media attention. By 1976, more than 1.4 million fans were attending races each year. In 1979, the Daytona 500 was televised nationwide for the first time. NASCAR was running at high speed—and poised to go even faster.

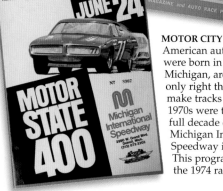

A BIG BOOST
This program from the 1972 championship season highlights NASCAR's first sponsor, which had joined the sport the year before. With the addition of the new name, the series' national profile rose dramatically.

MOTOR CITY
American automobiles were born in the Detroit, Michigan, area, so it was only right that NASCAR make tracks there. The 1970s were the first full decade of races at Michigan International Speedway in Detroit. This program is from the 1974 race.

A MOTOR SPORTS PIONEER
In 1977, Janet Guthrie became the first woman driver to start a Daytona 500, and finished in 12th place. In the same year, she was the first woman to race in the Indianapolis 500 with a team she owned and managed. Guthrie was later elected to the Women's Sports Hall of Fame. But she wasn't the first woman to take the wheel in NASCAR—Louise Smith ran a NASCAR Grand National race in 1949.

Doors were on their way out in the 1970s. For the first time, drivers entered stock cars through the window.

Long hood provides "crunch room" to protect the driver.

Main sponsor's logo

Secondary sponsor stickers

GOOD*YEAR*

Cale Yarborough

STP CHAMPION SPARK PLUGS

STP Regal Ride

NORRIS RACING WHEELS

GOODYEAR

Steel bumpers to absorb impact

Wide, slick racing tires

Petty vs. Pearson

In the 1970s, two great racers came head to head. In this legendary duel, Richard Petty came out on top in the record books with seven NASCAR NEXTEL Cup championships, but on the track, David Pearson was his constant rival. Their races against each other are among the most storied in NASCAR history. Petty finished his career with 200 victories. Pearson, with 105, comes second only to Petty for career race wins.

PEARSON'S POWERFUL PUROLATOR
David Pearson drove this No. 21 car during part of his extraordinary 1960–1986 career. The three-time NASCAR single-season champion won his only Daytona 500 victory in 1976.

Petty's Dodge Charger

OPEN FACE HELMET
Most driver's helmets in the 1970s were open faced, like this one—but the hard construction was an improvement from earlier leather models. Another helmet advance: an attached radio that let the driver talk to his team during a race.

Radio mouthpiece was attached with a metal arm to the outside of the helmet.

DUELING TITANS
Here in action from the 1976 Daytona 500 are four of the greatest drivers of all time. In order, they are Bobby Allison, David Pearson, Richard Petty, and A.J. Foyt. Petty and Pearson dueled down the stretch, but Pearson won the race despite a dramatic last-lap crash that spun him and Petty into the infield. Petty's car was too badly damaged to finish the race.

Pearson battled Allison for the lead during much of the historic race.

"CAM 2" is the brand of motor oil that sponsored Allison.

Caps feature team sponsors.

THREE-TIME CHAMP
South Carolina native Cale Yarborough was one of the all-time greatest drivers in NASCAR, winning 83 races and three championships in a career that spanned parts of four decades (1957–1988). He is the only driver to win titles in three consecutive years (1976 through 1978) and was runner-up on two other occasions. In 1977, he was named NASCAR Driver of the Year. Yarborough also won four Daytona 500s—that's a record second only to Richard Petty's total of seven.

THE ALABAMA GANG
That was the nickname for this successful trio of 1970s drivers: brothers Donnie and Bobby Allison, and Neil Bonnett (far right), all of whom hailed from Hueytown, Alabama. Between them, the trio won more than 100 NASCAR races. Bobby Allison's son Davey was also a member of the gang.

Fire-resistant drivers' uniform

The heavy metal and large size of cars of the 1970s were designed to keep driver's safe.

NASCAR NEXTEL CUP CHAMPIONS	
1970	Bobby Isaac
1971	Richard Petty
1972	Richard Petty
1973	Benny Parsons
1974	Richard Petty
1975	Richard Petty
1976	Cale Yarborough
1977	Cale Yarborough
1978	Cale Yarborough
1979	Richard Petty

The 1980s

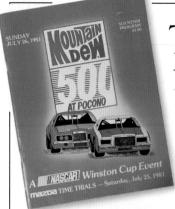

THE KING ON TV
The presence of television cameras at every NASCAR race accelerated throughout the decade. As more and more fans watched the races on TV, NASCAR's popularity started to spread beyond its original home in the South. Racing superstars like Richard Petty (above) became famous across the United States.

Bᴜɪʟᴅɪɴɢ ᴏɴ ᴛʜᴇ rapid growth of the 1970s, NASCAR kept the ride going strong in the 1980s. More and more fans began to enjoy the sport on TV, and by 1989, nearly every race in the top series was televised live nationwide. Many more national sponsors looked to NASCAR to help them sell their products. On the track, a new crop of stars came to prominence, led by Dale Earnhardt, who kicked off the decade with the first of his record-tying seven NASCAR NEXTEL Cup championships.

SPEED IN PENNSYLVANIA
This is a program from the 1981 Mountain Dew 400 held at Pocono Raceway in Long Pond, Pennsylvania. Beginning the next year, NASCAR held races at Pocono twice each season.

This souvenir newspaper highlighted Waltrip's win.

T-shirt honoring Darrell Waltrip

Championship trophy

DARRELL'S BIG NEWS
Darrell Waltrip won three titles in the 1980s. He celebrated his first in 1981 (earned with the help of 12 race wins) by showing off this mock headline.

THREE-TIMER
Darrell Waltrip became only the second driver ever to win three NASCAR NEXTEL Cup titles when he followed his 1981 title with championships in 1982 and 1985. This shirt features two of the car numbers he drove under in his career. Drivers occasionally change numbers if they change race teams.

BROTHER NUMBER ONE
Terry Labonte won the 1984 NASCAR NEXTEL Cup finishing in the top 10 in 24 races. He was the last champ to earn less than $1 million—today's victory pouch can exceed $9 million. When his brother Bobb earned the title in 2000, they became the first sibling to each win a NASCAR NEXTEL Cup Series title.

FINALLY A CHAMPION
Bobby Allison had a great NASCAR career, winning 84 races, among the most ever. He also won three Daytona 500s. In 1972, he won 10 races, but finished second overall to Richard Petty. In 1983, however, he finally pulled everything together. In addition to capturing six victories, he piled up enough points to capture his only NASCAR NEXTEL Cup championship, in this Buick.

AWESOME BILL FROM DAWSONVILLE

In 1987, Bill Elliott, a popular and successful driver from Dawsonville, Georgia, went faster in a stock car than anyone before or since. During qualifying for a race at Talladega 1987, Bill reached a top speed of 212 mph (341 km/h), which still stands as a NASCAR record. At left, Bill's bright red car is shown at the start of the 1987 Daytona 500, when he started on the pole and won (right).

Cup awarded at Riverside International Raceway

Elliott started on the pole and kept his lead.

Elliot's T-shirt sends a message to his mother.

WALLACE WAS A WINNER

Rusty Wallace, seen after a victory in Riverside, California, won the only season championship his long and successful career in 1989, edging out Dale Earnhardt by only 12 points.

MAN OF THE DECADE

Dale Earnhardt, here enjoying a congratulatory kiss from his wife Theresa, was the dominant driver of the 1980s. Dale won championships in 1980, 1986, and 1987. Known for his hard-charging style, he became one of the most beloved drivers ever.

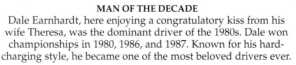

NASCAR NEXTEL CUP CHAMPIONS

1980	Dale Earnhardt
1981	Darrell Waltrip
1982	Darrell Waltrip
1983	Bobby Allison
1984	Terry Labonte
1985	Darrell Waltrip
1986	Dale Earnhardt
1987	Dale Earnhardt
1988	Bill Elliott
1989	Rusty Wallace

NASCAR in the 1990s

THE 1990S HAD A FAMILIAR ring to them right off the starting line: Dale Earnhardt carrying home the NASCAR championship trophy. "The Man in Black" continued the winning streak he had started in the 1980s. NASCAR continued to expand, adding sites and tracks. New television partners helped ratings skyrocket. Prize money jumped, too, with the overall winner receiving more than twice as much in 1999 as in 1990. The fans—and drivers— were loving the speed more than ever before.

DALE KEEPS ROLLING
After winning three titles in the 1980s, Dale Earnhardt kicked off the 1990s by winning two more. He added another pair in 1993 and 1994 to tie Richard Petty for most titles overall with seven. In 1990, he recorded four race wins and became the first driver to top the $3-million prize mark in one season.

Rusty won at least one race a year for 16 years in a row.

NEARLY THERE
In 1989, Rusty Wallace (right) had nipped Dale Earnhardt for the season title by only 12 points. In 1993, Earnhardt returned the favor, edging Wallace by only 80 points. Both drivers had two victories apiece, but although Wallace put together 19 top-five finishes, he didn't have enough total points to beat "The Intimidator."

SURPRISE WINNER
In 1992, Alan Kulwicki clinched this trophy for winning the NASCAR NEXTEL Cup championship. He was famous for driving his victory lap the wrong way around the track.

Modern "front clips" contain graphite composites to absorb energy in a crash.

PACKING THEM IN AT THE TRACKS
This enormous crowd of fans at Daytona International Speedway in 1993 was evidence of the enormous growth of NASCAR in the 1990s. Daytona, built in 1959, remained the most famous and popular track, but NASCAR added other tracks in the 1990s, including New Hampshire International Speedway (1993), California Speedway (1997), Las Vegas Motor Speedway (1998), and Homestead-Miami Speedway (1999).

A BIG NEW RACE
The 1994 debut of the Brickyard 400 marked the first NASCAR-sanctioned race at the Indianapolis Speedway.

THE KID COMES THROUGH

Most NASCAR champions earned their titles after many years of moving up in the ranks. In 1995, Jeff Gordon showed just how talented he was by zooming ahead of veteran drivers to win his first championship title after only three full years as a NASCAR driver. Gordon, known as "The Kid," went on to win seven races that year.

A colorfully clad Jeff Gordon starts his 1997 championship run with a victory.

Daytona 125 trophy for a shorter (125-mile) season-opening race

GOLDEN DOZEN

It had been 12 years since Terry Labonte reached the top of the NASCAR charts in the 1980s, and many thought he was past his prime. Labonte proved them wrong by winning his second championship in 1996.

DALE, JR. JOINS HIS DAD

NASCAR is famous for its families. In 1999, fans watched another family team up in the NASCAR NEXTEL Cup Series. Dale Earnhardt, Sr. was joined by his son Dale, Jr., who drove in five NASCAR NEXTEL Cup races in his debut year. Dale, Jr. was a third-generation NASCAR racer; Dale, Sr.'s father, Ralph, was also a top NASCAR driver.

NASCAR NEXTEL CUP CHAMPIONS	
1990	Dale Earnhardt, Sr.
1991	Dale Earnhardt, Sr.
1992	Alan Kulwicki
1993	Dale Earnhardt, Sr.
1994	Dale Earnhardt, Sr.
1995	Jeff Gordon
1996	Terry Labonte
1997	Jeff Gordon
1998	Jeff Gordon
1999	Dale Jarrett

ALWAYS A CONTENDER

Metal rails to direct airflow

Veteran driver Mark Martin (No. 6 car, below) was the model of consistency in the 1990s. He finished in the top 10 every season (in fact, in every season from 1989 through 2000). He finished second overall in three seasons in the 1990s (and again in 2002), and finished third three other seasons. Though Martin has never claimed the top spot at the end of a season, his knack of keeping in the running makes him a top driver.

Spoilers help keep the back end "tighter" to the track.

NASCAR today

SPRINGY SOUVENIR
NASCAR fans enjoy one of the widest range of souvenirs in sports, as shown by this Rusty Wallace bobblehead doll.

If FANS THOUGHT the first 50 years in NASCAR were great ones, in the new millennium, they learned that NASCAR could grow even bigger. With increased television exposure, a new series sponsor in 2004, and great racing action, NASCAR reached new heights of popularity. Attendance at the season's 36 points events topped 6.8 million only in the NASCAR NEXTEL Cup Series, while TV ratings had never been higher. The creation in 2004 of the "Chase for the NASCAR NEXTEL Cup" created even more excitement. NASCAR is roaring ahead in high gear.

WAY TO GO, BRO!
Terry Labonte had already brought two NASCAR NEXTEL Cup titles back home to the family in Texas. In 2000, brother Bobby added to the trophy case. With Bobby's championship to kick off the new millennium, the Labontes became the first pair of brothers to each win the sport's highest honor.

NASCAR DRIVERS LIGHT THE WAY
In the new millennium, NASCAR drivers enjoyed their widest popularity yet. They appeared in more and more commercials, and could be seen in many events away from the track. Here, driver Dale Jarrett takes part in the Olympic torch relay before the 2002 Winter Olympics in Salt Lake City.

Checker 500 trophy, shaped like the state of Arizona

Cartoon images of NASCAR drivers on car hood

GORDON KICKS OFF 'TOON TIME
Another way that NASCAR began to receive more notice in the wider media world was through the *NASCAR Racers* cartoon series. Here, Jeff Gordon poses with a car decorated with the *NASCAR Racers* logo.

NASCAR NEXTEL CUP CHAMPIONS	
2000	Bobby Labonte
2001	Jeff Gordon
2002	Tony Stewart
2003	Matt Kenseth
2004	Kurt Busch

ANOTHER YOUNG WINNER
In 2002, Matt Kenseth won five races, including the Checker Auto Parts 500, as shown at left. A year later, he won only one race, but ended up holding the most important trophy of all: the one that goes to the NASCAR season champion.

TONY THE TIGER

Tony Stewart is no stranger to winning. Before he joined the top ranks in NASCAR, he became the first driver ever to win three United States Auto Club titles in one year. He was also a former champion in go-karting. In Tony's first five seasons with NASCAR, he never finished lower than seventh. His best season came in 2002, when he won three races, more than $9 million, and the NASCAR NEXTEL Cup Series championship. As the 2000s roll forward, look for Tony to be in the hunt for more trophies.

Winners of NASCAR's top series received this trophy through 2003.

NEW FANS . . . NEW MARKETS

Along with adding races in new states, NASCAR has made a big splash on the media scene in recent years. Younger fans could see their heroes, such as Brian Vickers, on red scooter at right, racing against an MTV VJ, a development that NASCAR's founders would probably never have predicted.

MTV's Damien Fahey lost the scooter race.

NASCAR ROARS AHEAD IN THE 21ST CENTURY

ed by star drivers like Kurt Busch (front), NASCAR has come a long way om the beaches and dirt tracks of the 1940s. Buoyed by a growing fan ase and comprehensive television coverage, NASCAR has become merica's fastest-growing sport. Technology has improved the rs as well as made them much safer to drive, and hot young rivers are making headlines every week. One thing hasn't anged in all those years, however: Speed wins.

Transponder

Ryan Newman drafts behind Busch.

Hood pins

Headlight sticker

The stock car

THE CENTERPIECE OF NASCAR is the "stock car," which is the type of race car driven in NASCAR. Stock means that the car's body type is modeled after a regular passenger car; that is, cars kept in a car dealer's "stock." At first, stock cars were actually passenger cars made over for racing. Today's stock car, a high-tech combination of speed, science, and safety, is built just for racing, but it's still modeled after passenger car types.

Early cars had glass windshields and doors that worked.

Using "real" cars is grea[t] advertising fo[r] car makers

HOMEGROWN
The first stock cars were not "modeled" after passenge[r] cars—they actually *were* passenger cars! This race photo from 1957 shows a Hudson Horne[t] (front) and a Chevrolet (back), both taken fro[m] the home garage to the track (with a stop for some paint and some increased engine power). Cars back then were heavier, larger, and harder to steer.

IN THE COCKPIT
Stock cars have specialized dashboards that are far different from what you see in your family car. The white dials on the dash tell the driver about engine functions such as oil pressure and battery power. The dials are turned so that when everything is working right, the indicators point straight up.

Ignition kill switch

Main switch panel

Rear view mirror

Safety seat

Head and neck restraint

Gauges that monitor various engine functions

Extra switches for fans or ignition

Master switch shuts down electrical system in emergency situations

Radio button

Gearshift

Fire extinguisher

Seat belt harness

Fire extinguisher switch

STAR OF THE SHO[W]
Colorful, powerful, made [by] teams of experts, and driven by [a] daring pro, today's stock car [is] the most recognizable part [of] NASCAR racing. Cars a[re] carefully regulated for safe[ty] and fairness. They must wei[gh] at least 3,400 lbs (1,542 kg). Ea[ch] car is 200.7 in (5 m) long, 51 (1.2 m) high, and 72.5 in (1.8 [m] at its widest poin[t].

NASCAR cars don't have lights; these are just stickers.

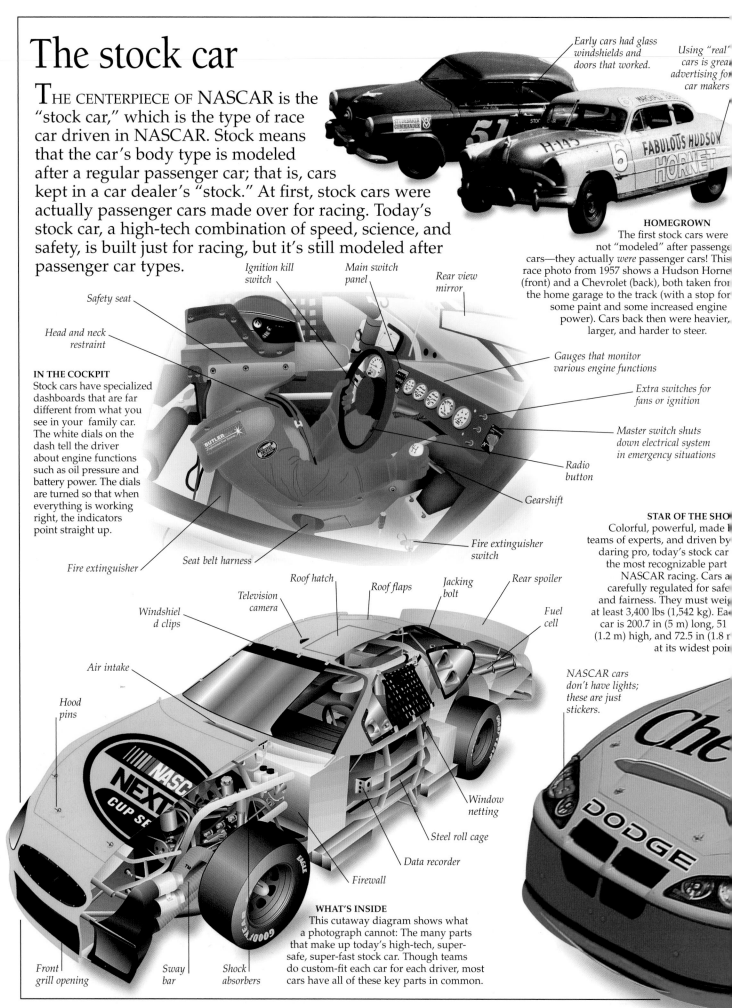

Roof hatch

Roof flaps

Jacking bolt

Rear spoiler

Television camera

Fuel cell

Windshiel d clips

Air intake

Hood pins

Window netting

Steel roll cage

Data recorder

Firewall

Front grill opening

Sway bar

Shock absorbers

WHAT'S INSIDE
This cutaway diagram shows what a photograph cannot: The many parts that make up today's high-tech, super-safe, super-fast stock car. Though teams do custom-fit each car for each driver, most cars have all of these key parts in common.

Part of head-and-neck restraint

Solid steel frame

Head restraint bars

Sponsors' advertisement

SIEMENS

SEE YOUR LOCAL DODGE DEALER

DODGE

19

Bolts for adjusting spoiler

REAR VIEW
The design of stock cars is aimed at making them move through the air smoothly as they speed around the track. The black bar shown above helps keep the car from slipping on the track. Air passing over the bar creates a downward pressure.

SIMPSON

High sides reduce movement

WHERE'S THE DOOR?
NASCAR vehicles do not have doors. Drivers have to climb in through window openings. Having no doors means that a complete, hinge-free steel roll cage can be built to protect the driver.

Straps adjust here

Five-point, quick-release safety harness made of heavy-duty nylon webbing.

SITTING FOR SAFETY
The drivers' seats have perhaps evolved more than any other part of stock-car technology. The seats start with this all-steel frame, molded to contain a driver as tightly, and thus as safely, as possible. Slots are made to allow for additional safety straps. On top of the steel frame, car makers put thin padding molded to each drivers' body. They drivers will be sitting for as long as four hours in a hot car, so they want to be comfortable.

The team's top sponsor gets the prime position on the hood of the car.

Metal roof strips direct airflow to help prevent rollovers.

The car's number is painted on the roof and the sides.

The rear spoiler helps direct the car's air flow, reducing the tendency to lift off the road at high speeds.

43

JEFF GREEN

STP

WINN DIXIE

OLD EL PASO

MBNA

NEXTEL

OUTBACK

Holley

GOODYEAR

WM

MAC TOOLS

EA SPORTS

JESEL   Mobil 1

43

43

FERGUSON

LINCOLN WELDERS

MSD 3M

Autolite   Mobil 1

Plexiglass side windows have openings to create better air flow.

Race cars have no side mirrors. A large mirror inside the car helps drivers see behind them.

Nylon webbing covers the drivers' window area.

All NASCAR race cars run on treadless Goodyear tires.

21

Building the stock car

YOUR FAMILY'S CAR WAS BUILT on an assembly line, an exact copy of every other car of the same model. But the cars driven in NASCAR races are all hand-crafted individually. Car makers spend millions of dollars and thousands of hours working to create better, faster, and more efficient designs. Though each team must work within NASCAR rules on a list of standard body types, within those rules expertise and creativity make a big difference. These pictures show the steps of car making, from the initial ideas of a designer to the finishing touches of the painter. It takes many weeks—and many hands—to make a winning car.

TESTING, TESTING
A prototype car's construction is tested for crash safety, and its materials for sturdiness at the NASCAR Research and Development Center in Concord, North Carolina.

STEP ONE: COMPUTERS
A variety of computer programs allow car designers to try different plans for the chassis, or frame, of the race car. On this computer screen, the chassis is shown by white lines.

STEP TWO: MATERIALS
Steel is the primary component of the metal skeleton that forms the basic shape of each car. The steel begins as hollow rods, tubes, or beams. Using the plan created by the designer, workers weld the steel together.

STEP THREE: BUILDING THE CHASSIS AND THE ROLL CAGE
The car begins to take its shape with the steel tubes that create the sides of the chassis, and the round tubes bent into place to form the roof. Together, they form a roll cage to surround and protect the driver. The front of the car and the engine housing can also be seen.

Frame to support chassis during assembly

Steel tubes support roof and top of roll cage.

A strong roll cage is essential for protecting the driver.

STEP FOUR: ADDING THE PARTS
With the roll cage and basic shape formed, additional parts, some made of sheet metal, are added to the chassis construction. The thick steel firewall divides the engine compartment from the driver's seating area.

Bar removed after construction.

Sidebars protect driver.

Curved metal forms wheel well.

Tires hung during construction are not race tires.

STEP FIVE: METAL FABRICATION

Once the steel chassis has been formed and welded, the metal fabricators get to work. Using very precise measurements created by the computer designers, experts called "fabricators" bend, mold, shape, and press sheets of metal around the chassis.

IN A CRUNCH

The metal fabricators who work so hard to shape the car's shell hate pictures like this. A crash during a race has crumpled the metal like paper. However, the hard steel chassis has kept its shape, protecting driver Tony Stewart.

Clips holding metal sheets together will be removed prior to final grinding and smoothing of this outer metal skin.

Window opening

Solid steel panels wrap around front and sides of chassis.

Area left open to install air dam later.

Windshield made of high-impact plastic

Hood clips hold the hood down instead of interior latches.

Heavy bars will support engine.

STEP SIX: MAKING IT BEAUTIFUL

After the metal fabricators have done their job, the entire outside of the car is sanded and buffed until it is perfectly smooth. Several coats of paint, as well as any specialized decals, designs, or logos, are then added. This outside of the car is the body and it sits on the chassis. It can be removed easily to install other parts of the car such as electronics, seats, and other interior gear.

Firewall separates driver and engine.

Engine compartment

Adjustable rear spoilers

Brake lights

Metal strips support windshield

VIEW FROM THE BACK

This rear-view of the car shows the steel roll cage through the back window. The black tab atop the rear deck is a spoiler that helps control air flow over the car during a race. The entire process of designing the chassis is aimed at creating the most aerodynamic shape possible for the car to cut through the wind. The spoiler shown here helps the air "push" the car down on the race track.

SEE YOUR LOCAL
DODGE DEALER

DODGE

Engines

DRIVERS MAKE NASCAR VEHICLES GO, but the powerful engines provide the push. The eight-cylinder engines in NASCAR NEXTEL Cup cars can produce over 800 horsepower, about four times as much as standard passenger cars. The engines can be betweeen two and three times larger than a typical four-cylinder passenger-car engine. While NASCAR teams must follow rules about engine building, they often "tinker" to pull all the power they can from their engines.

CAREFUL INSPECTION
Although engines are carefully assembled prior to arriving at race tracks, some parts can be added or swapped out. Here a crew member inspects spark plugs with a loupe.

Cylinder for piston

ENGINE BLOCK
The main part of the engine is the cast-iron engine block. (NASCAR uses small block engines.) The circular holes are four of the eight cylinders into which the piston move to make the engine turn and the wheels move. In this partially assembled engine, the piston on the far right is not yet in place.

CAMSHAFT ON TOP
While the crankshaft (below) is pushed around by the pistons, the camshaft (left) pushes the valves up and down from a position above them.

MAKING SPARKS
Spark plugs like these cause small explosions on top of the pistons. Repeatedly emitting a small spark, the plugs ignite the air-gasoline mixture inside each piston's cylinder.

Valve spring

SPRINGING INTO ACTION
Atop the pistons are valve springs such as this one, which pop up and down with each piston stroke with the help of the camshaft. Opening and closing, the valves let air and fuel into the cylinders and then let exhaust gases out.

Valve

Piston

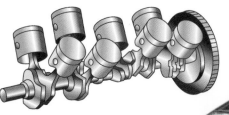

V-8 CYLINDER DIAGRAM
This diagram shows the arrangement of the eight pistons on the crankshaft. Each pair of pistons forms a "V" shape as they move up and down inside the engine block, which is why engines of this type are called "V-8s." More pistons means more power—thus a V-8 can move a car faster than a four-cylinder.

Crankpin

Link to starter

PISTONS
Making the crankshafts revolve is the job of the pistons. There are eight of these pistons in a NASCAR engine. The crankshaft fits inside the hole at the bottom.

Connecting rod

CRANK IT UP
Car engines work by turning crankshafts, which turn the car's axles and wheels. NASCAR-quality crankshafts such as this one are designed to handle more than 9,000 revolutions (or turns) per minute (RPM), or more than 150 per second!

Oil pump

Induction: piston descending, intake valve open, exhaust valve closed

Compression: piston rising, intake and exhaust valves closed

Power: piston descending, intake and exhaust valves closed

Exhaust: piston rising, intake valve closed, exhaust valve open

THE FOUR-STROKE CYCLE
Each piston goes through four phases, which taken together make up two strokes of the piston. In the chamber above the piston, gas, air, and a spark combine to create a small explosion, which powers the movement of the piston in the cylinder, making it go up and down.

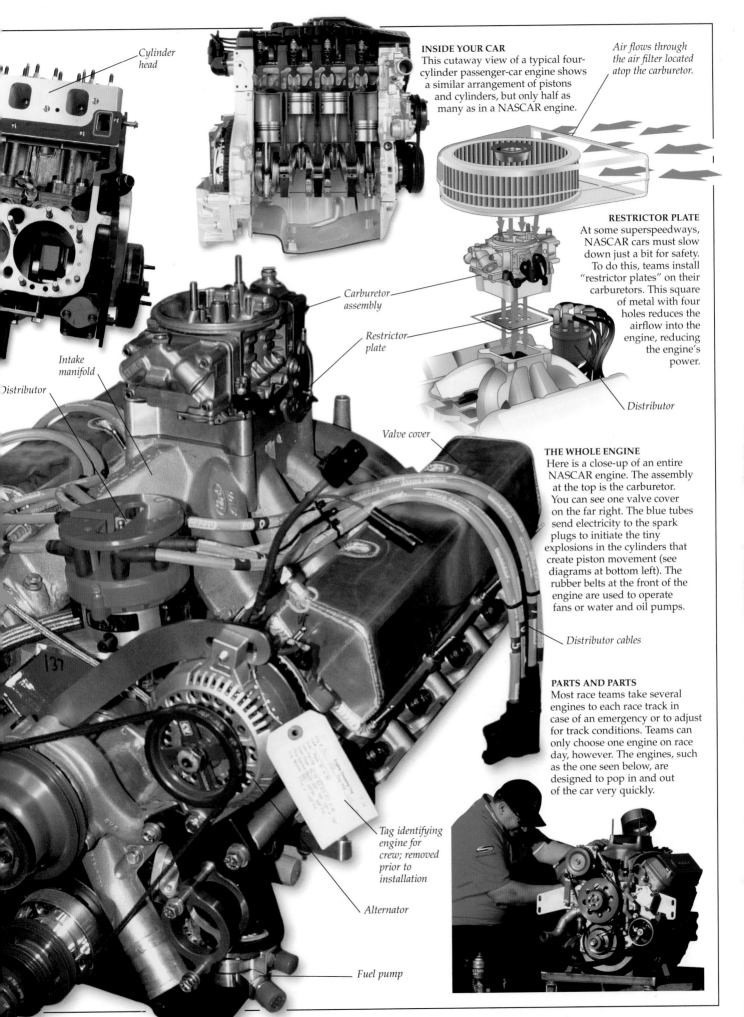

Cylinder head

INSIDE YOUR CAR
This cutaway view of a typical four-cylinder passenger-car engine shows a similar arrangement of pistons and cylinders, but only half as many as in a NASCAR engine.

Air flows through the air filter located atop the carburetor.

RESTRICTOR PLATE
At some superspeedways, NASCAR cars must slow down just a bit for safety. To do this, teams install "restrictor plates" on their carburetors. This square of metal with four holes reduces the airflow into the engine, reducing the engine's power.

Carburetor assembly

Restrictor plate

Distributor

Distributor

Intake manifold

Valve cover

THE WHOLE ENGINE
Here is a close-up of an entire NASCAR engine. The assembly at the top is the carburetor. You can see one valve cover on the far right. The blue tubes send electricity to the spark plugs to initiate the tiny explosions in the cylinders that create piston movement (see diagrams at bottom left). The rubber belts at the front of the engine are used to operate fans or water and oil pumps.

Distributor cables

PARTS AND PARTS
Most race teams take several engines to each race track in case of an emergency or to adjust for track conditions. Teams can only choose one engine on race day, however. The engines, such as the one seen below, are designed to pop in and out of the car very quickly.

Tag identifying engine for crew; removed prior to installation

Alternator

Fuel pump

All about tires

WHERE THE RUBBER MEETS THE ROAD—or the track—tires are a critical component of the race car. More attention is paid to the tires than just about any other part of the car. The tires have to withstand high temperatures and top speeds. They must also provide the right traction for the track and weather conditions. Although every team uses the same kind of official tires, each team decides when to change those tires, how much air to put in them, how much wear and tear they want to put on them, and which type of tire to use on which track—choices that often make the difference between winning and losing.

Rubber surface is flat and smooth.

Surface has ridges and grooves.

Racing tire

Street tire

RACING TIRES VS. STREET TIRES
These side-by-side illustrations show how NASCAR racing tires are different from passenger-car tires. Racing tires cost more than twice as much, but won't last more than one race day, while street tires last for a few years.

RIMS AT THE READY
Although you only hear them called "tires" around the track, the tires are actually complete wheels, made up of a rubber exterior and these metal rims, stacked here awaiting pre-race assembly.

COUNTING UP TIRE
Each team is given sets of tires by NASCAR's official tire supplier, Goodyear. Team members then check them in, carefully marking and counting the tires and preparing them for the car.

Air nozzle connects to valve on rim.

Gauge measures up to 100 psi (pounds per square inch).

UNDER PRESSURE
Tires are filled with air under pressure. This device measures the amont of pressure in each tire, which is vital information for the racing team. Tire pressure affects car handling and traction and tire durability.

Rubber hose

PUTTING ON AIR
Crew members carefully check the air pressure in each tire before a race begins. Teams will keep tires at varying pressures on hand to allow for different racing conditions.

SMOKIN' HOT VICTORY!
After winning a race, drivers will often rev up their engines and purposely make their tires spin so fast that they smoke and leave thick tire marks on the track. This has become part of the victory celebration. Kurt Busch is seen here spinning his wheels after winning a 2004 race at Bristol Motor Speedway.

Only the front wheels on a NASCAR car can turn, as on a regular passenger car.

Unused tire   Used tire

HARD-WORKING TIRES

This pair of tires shows just how much damage a race can do to a tire. The rubber of the tires heats up during a race and slowly peels or breaks off. Also, the slick-faced tires pick up debris on the track, usually rubber from other cars' tires. This level of wear is the main reason that cars and crews change tires so often during a race.

Blowout possibly caused by debris cutting the rubber

CUT DOWN

NASCAR racing is tough on tires. The tire wall is only ⅛-inch (3-mm) thick, and the air inside it is under pressure. If a patch of rubber wears out, the pressure can blow a hole in the tire, which is not an easy feat considering the durability of these tires.

Changing tires

During a race, the pit crew will change a car's tires anywhere from four to six times. They actually change the whole wheel, including the steel rim, but the assembly is always called the tire. Tires wear down during a race, so fresh tires can mean more speed and better handling.

AIR GUN

Powered by compressed air, this special tool is used by the pit crew members known as tire changers. They can remove five lug nuts (below) in about two seconds.

LUG NUTS

Each wheel is attached to the axle by five hexagonal lug nuts. They are sometimes lightly glued to the wheels before the race to make tightening easier.

Crews use code numbers and letters to label tires.

GOING UP!

The jack man puts a jack (with yellow handle, above) under one side of the car, pushes down on the lever, and raises the side of the car slightly off the ground. This elevates the tires and allows the tire changers to take off the lug nuts and remove the entire wheel.

WHEELY GOOD

This photo shows the arrangement of the five lug nuts at the center of the rim. The tire itself is attached to the outside of that rim.

Drivers only make skidmarks when they are sure they will not be using the tires again.

Colors and numbers

Fᴿᴼᴹ ᴛʜᴇ ᴍᴜʟᴛɪᴄᴏʟᴏʀᴇᴅ ᴅʀɪᴠᴇʀ's ᴜɴɪғᴏʀᴍs to the distinctive paint schemes of the cars, NASCAR racing is one of the sports world's most colorful spectacles. Photos from the early days of stock-car racing show dark-colored cars marked with white numbers and drivers in plain clothing. Today, cars race in a blaze of vivid colors. The colors of today's cars are an important part of NASCAR buisness, and make watching the races much more interesting. Car numbers, meanwhile, identify drivers and become as well known as their names.

A SWEET SPONSORSHIP DEAL
The biggest source of color in NASCAR today comes from the designs created for cars by sponsors. This number-38 M&Ms Ford Taurus driven by Elliott Sadler in 2004 is one of the more colorful ones. Sponsors pay fees to racing teams to feature their logos, products, and advertisements on their car. The main team sponsor controls the hood and sides of the cars. Secondary sponsors add stickers.

SHOWING OFF THE UNIFORMS
NASCAR cars are certainly colorful (below), but the drivers themselves also resemble brightly colored walking billboards. This photo shows the ten drivers who qualified for the 2004 Chase for the NASCAR NEXTEL Cup, posing with the trophy itself. Check out the wide array of colors, designs, and logos. Note that some drivers might change uniforms from year to year as sponsors change.

Dale Earnhardt Jr.

Jeff Gordon

Jimmie Johnson

Tony Stewart

Matt Kenseth

Jeremy Mayfield

Kurt Busch

Mark Martin

Ryan Newman

Elliott Sadler

Service members stand at attention.

U.S. Marines logo

The logo or name of a service branch is on each car hood.

Driver Greg Biffle

Driver Bobby Hamilton Jr.

Numbers in action

ach NASCAR vehicle is identifed with a number, hared with its driver. During a racing season, no two ehicles can share the same number. However, a few f the same numbers have been used by different rivers throughout NASCAR history. Numbers are ontrolled by a team owner and assigned to his team's ars, regardless of who is driving. A team might ontrol several numbers t one time.

Dust flies during skid.

Cale Yarborough, 1975–1980

Ned Jarrett, 1960s

Sign for Kevin Harvick's team

NUMBERS AT WORK
Large numbered signs are used by pit crews to identify their pit road space for drivers. The signs here are part of the colorful pre-race ceremonies.

HISTORY OF NUMBER 11
s an example of how a umber has been shared by table drivers, these four otos show various number-11 rs through the years. (Bill Elliott so drove a number 11 from 1992 to 94.) In 2005, that number is owned y the Joe Gibbs racing team, with young son Leffler as the driver. e's sure to follow in the re tracks of these great umber-11 racers.

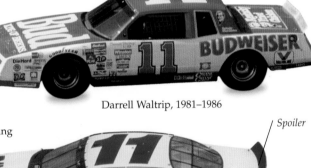

Darrell Waltrip, 1981–1986

Spoiler

Todd Bodine, 1995–2003

SHOWING THEIR COLORS
Many fans love to show off their loyalty to a driver by displaying his colors and number, as this Jeff Gordon souvenir car flag shows.

U.S. Coast Guard logo

U.S. Air Force logo

Driver Casey Atwood

Driver Joe Nemechek

Driver Justin Labonte

Driver Ricky Rudd

WAR PAINT
In 2004, these six cars ran in various NASCAR races with special paint schemes that honored the branches of the U.S. military. These are examples of the NASCAR practice of creating specially-painted cars for special purposes, rather than for a sponsor. NASCAR fans have expressed a great interest in patriotism over the years, so this promotion was very well received.

Drivers' gear

LIKE TOP ATHLETES in any sport, NASCAR drivers use the latest high-tech equipment when they compete—not just for speed on the track, but also for comfort and protection in the driver's seat. As these pictures show, some equipment has changed over time. New materials and designs have made everything from helmets to shoes safer and more comfortable. These days, each driver's gear is custom-made to fit him perfectly, and specially designed to do a specific job to protect him. All this technology is aimed at keeping drivers safe, so they can focus on one thing: winning.

Car number painted on side of helmet

1950s

Replica of driver's signature

Nylon webbing chin strap

Foam padding to mold to the driver's head

1980s

High impact plastic face shield

2004

PROTECTION UP TOP
Drivers' helmets are among the most important pieces of safety equipment—and among the most high-tech. In the early years of racing, they looked like little more than construction hard hats. Today's helmets are made of heavy-duty plastics and kevlar, and include shatterproof faceguards and built in cooling and radio systems.

EARLY DRIVER GEAR
In NASCAR's early days, driver gear was a far cry from today's high-tech uniforms. Many drivers, such as Tim Flock, above, wore only a jacket, shirt, and jeans to race. As the sport grew, drivers and race teams learned to make more of uniforms—for both safety and advertising.

FASHION AND FUNCTION
A colorful racing uniform is a key part of a driver's gear. Jumpsuits are better for the seated drivers than shirt and pants, as the shirts would ride up their back. Seven-time NASCAR NEXTEL Cup champion Richard Petty wore this nylon, STP-logoed jumpsuit in the 1970s.

High collar for snug fit

Primary sponsor logo is front and center

Petty's sunglasses, not worn while racing

Epaulets are for style only

Secondary sponsors have small patches

Clamps attach the harness to brackets in the car

Buit-in belt is secured with velcro

Car number

SCIENCE EQUALS SAFETY
At top speeds, a driver experiences poweful G-forces; that is, while a car zooms around a turn, a driver is pressed back in his seat like an astronaut going up in a rocket. In an accident, a driver's head and neck can also move around dangerously. To help prevent injuries in these situations, all drivers wear this HANS (head and neck safety) device. It straps to their helmet, uniform, and car seat to create a cocoon of protection.

Side panels name racing team and sponsor

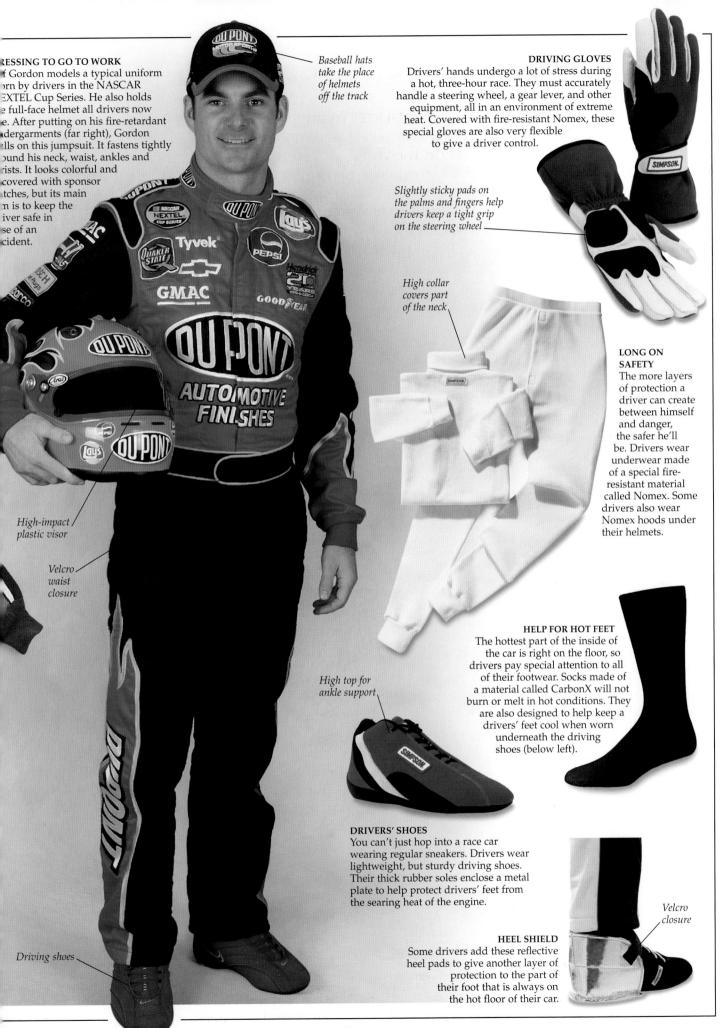

RESSING TO GO TO WORK
f Gordon models a typical uniform
orn by drivers in the NASCAR
EXTEL Cup Series. He also holds
e full-face helmet all drivers now
e. After putting on his fire-retardant
dergarments (far right), Gordon
lls on this jumpsuit. It fastens tightly
ound his neck, waist, ankles and
rists. It looks colorful and
covered with sponsor
tches, but its main
n is to keep the
iver safe in
se of an
cident.

*Baseball hats
take the place
of helmets
off the track*

*High-impact
plastic visor*

*Velcro
waist
closure*

Driving shoes

DRIVING GLOVES
Drivers' hands undergo a lot of stress during
a hot, three-hour race. They must accurately
handle a steering wheel, a gear lever, and other
equipment, all in an environment of extreme
heat. Covered with fire-resistant Nomex, these
special gloves are also very flexible
to give a driver control.

*Slightly sticky pads on
the palms and fingers help
drivers keep a tight grip
on the steering wheel*

*High collar
covers part
of the neck*

**LONG ON
SAFETY**
The more layers
of protection a
driver can create
between himself
and danger,
the safer he'll
be. Drivers wear
underwear made
of a special fire-
resistant material
called Nomex. Some
drivers also wear
Nomex hoods under
their helmets.

HELP FOR HOT FEET
The hottest part of the inside of
the car is right on the floor, so
drivers pay special attention to all
of their footwear. Socks made of
a material called CarbonX will not
burn or melt in hot conditions. They
are also designed to help keep a
drivers' feet cool when worn
underneath the driving
shoes (below left).

*High top for
ankle support*

DRIVERS' SHOES
You can't just hop into a race car
wearing regular sneakers. Drivers wear
lightweight, but sturdy driving shoes.
Their thick rubber soles enclose a metal
plate to help protect drivers' feet from
the searing heat of the engine.

*Velcro
closure*

HEEL SHIELD
Some drivers add these reflective
heel pads to give another layer of
protection to the part of
their foot that is always on
the hot floor of their car.

At the track

YOU CAN'T HAVE A RACE WITHOUT A TRACK. Today's tracks come in all shapes and sizes, from long superspeedways to tight-turning road courses. Each track offers a different challenge for drivers—from the high speeds used on a superspeedway to the tight turns of a smaller oval track. With cars and crews, transport trucks, track officials, and safety workers, a NASCAR track on race day becomes as busy as a crowded city.

Lap number

Car numbers in racing order

WHO'S IN FIRST?
Fans at a track can keep "track" of the action by checking these light towers, usually located on the infield. The numbers show the cars during the race in their ever-changing running order.

WORKING AT THE TRACK
A large number of people work at each track during a race, from ticket sellers to food workers. Safety professionals, such as these tow truck drivers, are ready to deal with any emergency on or off the track. Here, a track tow truck removes Kasey Kahne's car after a wreck.

White lines indicate beginning, middle, and end of turns to help drivers gauge position on track.

The track apron is the paved portion of a racetrack that separates the racing surface from the infield.

In the track's four turns, the surface of the track is tilted or "banked" to help cars grip the track as they turn.

ALABAMA CLASSIC
A field of cars races by, too fast for the camera to capture, in this scene from Talladega Superspeedway in Alabama. Built in 1969 and still NASCAR's longest track at 2.66 miles (4.2 km) around, Talladega has been the scene of some of the most famous races in NASCAR history.

Drivers try to find a "groove" on each track, a route around the track that will let them maintain the highest possible speed.

Four track types

These diagrams show four typical track shapes. Superspeedways are at least a mile (1.6 km) in length and allow the fastest speeds. Short tracks are less than a mile (1.6 km) around; they have tighter turns and the traffic in a race there is much tighter. Road courses have plenty of twists and turns.

Pit road

Start/finish

Superspeedway
(This example is also called a "trioval.")

Pit road

Start/finish

Standard oval

Pit road

Start/finish

Tight turns

Short track

TWISTS AND TURNS
Drivers make only left-hand turns on three of the track types shown (all races are run counterclockwise). However, on road courses (right), drivers have to make right and left turns, along with powering down long straightaways. This type of racing is challenging for drivers used to racing on ovals.

Start/finish

Pit road

Road course

Turns in a road course can be as tight as 90 degrees.

Truck transports, which teams use to carry cars and gear from race to race, are parked on the infield.

This tower, equivalent to a scoreboard in other sports, monitors the race running order.

In the garage area, celebrities, politicians, and race teams can be seen before and after the race.

ROUND AND ROUND THEY GO
Bristol Motor Speedway is a favorite for many NASCAR fans. More than 150,000 people pack into the half-mile track to watch some great racing action. The tight turns and short course make each Bristol race a tightly contested one.

Pit road area where pit crews are stationed

Start-finish line

Flag station at start-finish line, next to and above track

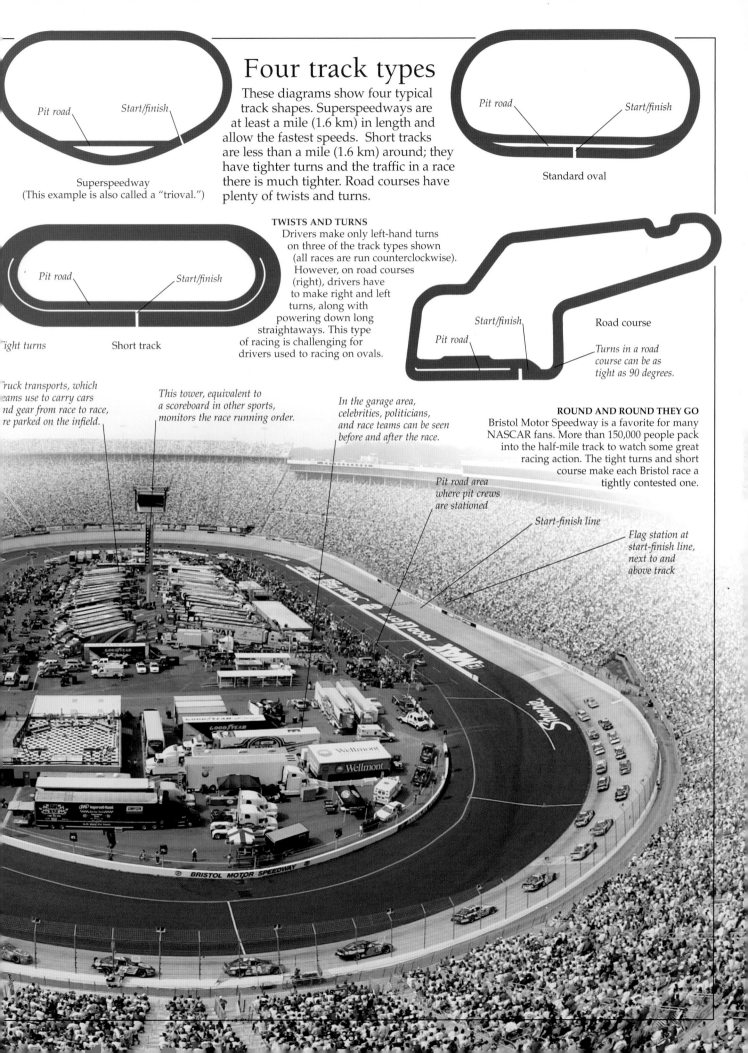

In the garage

Fans love the speed of NASCAR races, but the real action starts in team garages. Racing teams have garages at their headquarters where they prepare the cars before each race. To each race site, they also bring most of their garage with them—tools, parts, mechanics, and all. Adjustments may be made depending on weather conditions, track layout, and other factors, so teams bring all the tools they need to make tiny, precise adjustments or major engine or body repairs. The garage area on a track's infield, where all the teams work to make their car just that much faster than the others.

OLD TIME GARAGE WORK
The garage has always been the starting point for NASCAR success. This photo from 1960 shows ace driver and future championship owner Junior Johnson (center) and his crew at work. Though early NASCAR garage crews were expert mechanics, they didn't have all the advantages of technology enjoyed by today's racing teams.

FLYING SPARKS
The war wagon acts as anchor to all kinds of tasks. The workman above is using a grinding tool on a part held in the red clamp.

Utility clamps

Workbench area

Racks keep often-used tools handy.

TEAM "WAR WAGON"
Each team customizes a rolling "war wagon" like this one, filling it with tools, parts, wires, batteries, and all the other equipment they might need when they get to the track.

Spare batteries for hand tools or tanks for welding can be placed in this area.

Storage areas for parts

Adjustable rack area can be customized for each team's needs.

Plastic bins hold odds and ends.

Rubber tires

Fuel cans

Needlenose tip

Vertical storage area

Battery charging station for handheld drills

Racks will be filled with trays of tools.

Teams keep wrenches of all sizes for use on many parts of the car.

TOUGH TOOLS
NASCAR tools are made of heavy steel and high-impact plastic to stand up to hard work at the garage or the track.

Steel shaft

Holes at end of wrench are sized for standard nuts.

Screwdriver

Pliers

Portion of wrench set

EXPERT HELP
Drivers such as Jimmie Johnson (at left) are invaluable members of the garage-area team. The drivers' instructions help the team "set up" the car; that is, adjust the suspension and steering properly for each track's unique conditions.

Elastic nylon straps help hold the cover in place.

UP ON BLOCKS
When teams work on the brakes, they remove the wheels and put the car up on the orange, pyramid-shaped jacks. This gives them constant, easy access to these important parts of the car.

With tire removed, brake assembly is revealed.

Stacks of tires are often kept near the garage area.

UNDER WRAPS FOR PROTECTION
When a car leaves the garage to be placed on pit road and prepare for the start of the race, it is often covered. The front cover keeps the air intake grill from becoming clogged. During the race this grill lets in air that cools the engine. The windshield cover helps keep the inside of the car from becoming too hot in the sun.

ONE BUSY PLACE
Behind the scenes at a NASCAR race: Here is the garage area at Phoenix International Raceway. Tires are stacked by team areas. Mechanics, drivers, and car owners work on their cars. And fuel cans stand ready when needed.

Media members and race fans with special passes can sometimes go into the garage area.

Jack for lifting up side of car

Flags and judges

NASCAR HAS CREATED A LONG list of rules and regulations that, if followed, ensure that competition is safe, fair, and even. A large team of officials works at each race and behind the scenes in the NASCAR offices to make sure everyone follows those rules. Some rules cover how cars and engines are made, and inspectors check cars before each race. Other rules define how cars should move on and around the racetrack. Drivers who break the rules can be penalized in laps, points, or monetary fines. But everyone involved aims for a safe, fair race.

ENGINE CHECK
A pre-race inspection team checks out every part of the car, including the engine (above). NASCAR rules are designed to ensure fair competition, and these automotive experts carefully examine cars to make sure they comply with all the rules. Engines, for instance, must be of a certain size and must only contain parts approved in advance by NASCAR.

Protective gloves

Each official is assigned a specific position on race day.

GETTING STARTED
This group of NASCAR officials is on hand to get the cars lined up on the track before a race. Helping to "direct traffic" in the crowded garage and pit areas is an important saftey role for officials.

Hand signals help direct traffic or signal drivers and crew

Goggles

Ear-protecting radio headphones

Radio to speak with officials in the pit area and the booths above the track

Notepad with track and race information

Plastic visor

OFFICIAL'S HELMET
Even though officials don't drive in the race, they are still exposed to hazards such as flying debris and loud noise. All officials wear high-impact plastic helmets like this one, made to fit over headphones (below).

Handset clips to belt.

Yellow caution flag

Mouthpiece

OFFICIAL UNIFORM
Unlike drivers, officials wear plain white jumpsuits made for both comfort and safety.

CHECKING THE BODYWORK
This picture shows one of the metal "templates" used to make sure that all the cars conform to approved NASCAR body types. A variation as small as a fraction of an inch can send a car back to the garage to be fixed.

Sign gives running time of race.

FLAG MAN
This booth is built on the side of the track above the start-finish line. Officials climb a ladder to get inside, where they wave flags (below) alerting drivers of various race conditions.

Blue with yellow stripe: alerts drivers to let lead-lap cars pass

Yellow: caution flag, drivers must slow and not pass

White: lead driver's last lap

Checkered: waved as the winner crosses finish line

Green: start of race

Red: race is stopped

Black: driver is penalized

NASCAR NEXTEL Cup logo

CROSSING GUARD
White-suited NASCAR officials like this one help keep order, especially on the pit road. Using signs, hand signals, and radios, they help drivers avoid accidents. They also watch for pit stop rules violations.

Rubber-soled shoes help prevent slipping on oil or other race debris.

FLAGGING THE RACES
This entryway at Texas Motor Speedway displays the seven special signal flags that are waved by officials at various times during a race to help control the action. Officials also alert drivers and teams via radio about any situation on the track, such as an oil spill or an accident, or a weather issue. The checkered flag, of course, is the one that all the drivers want to see.

Welcome to TEXAS MOTOR SPEEDWAY

NASCAR fans

Early NASCAR fans lived mostly in the Southeastern United States, where the sport was born. Today, however, tens of millions of race fans live all over the country and around the world. NASCAR even held a race in Mexico in 2005. More than 13 million people attended NASCAR races at all levels in 2004, some making each race a family vacation—arriving for qualifying laps and practice, and staying through the weekend. Meanwhile, TV ratings grow annually. NASCAR fans are loyal to their favorite drivers, and drivers respond by being ready to meet fans. America is on the road to becoming a NASCAR nation!

CAN'T DO IT WITHOUT THEM
During every NASCAR weekend, savvy and patient fan know that they'll get several chances for autographs from their favorites, such as Matt Kenseth (above). NASCAR drivers have a great relationship with their fans, and often sponsor online fan clubs.

CLOSE TO THE ACTION
This 1955 convertible race (the car on the right is actually going backward after a spin out) shows how early fans enjoyed an up-close and personal view of the dirt-track NASCAR action. Not every track had enough seats or grandstands for fans to sit in, so they crowded along the edges of the infield area to watch the racing action.

EAR PROTECTION
The noise of roaring engines and cheering crowds can really build up during a typical NASCAR race. To protect their ears, many fans (and others at the track) wear special protective earphones. Some of these earphones also function as radios that fans can use to listen in to on-track radio chatter.

Hard plas earphones ha rubber ear rings create a tight f

SHOWING THEIR TRUE COLORS
Like other sports fans, NASCAR fans proudly wear the colors or numbers of their favorite drivers as they attend races. This shot above turns 3 and 4 at Bristol shows a great fans-eye view, as well as a sign of this fan's loyalty to racing legend Dale Earnhardt, Jr.

Race fans may remove their caps or hats during the playing of the National Anthem.

AMERICAN RACE FANS
NASCAR fans are very patriotic. Before each race, fans stand and sing along with the National Anthem. Then it's time to shout for their favorite drivers and cheer on the racing action.

TRAILER FANS
A unique feature of NASCAR races is the arrival, on Thursday, Friday, and Saturday of race weekend, of an army of mobile homes. Fans create temporary NASCAR fan "villages" on the infield of larger tracks, enjoying each other's company along with close-up views of the racing action. The mobile homes host big parties, barbecues, and celebrations.

These #3 flags honor the late Dale Earnhardt, Sr.

Souvenirs

NASCAR fans may be sports' most devoted souvenir shoppers. They can find their favorite driver's picture or his car, colors, or number on just about anything you can think of. Seen here are just a few items NASCAR fans collect to show their loyalty.

Race T-shirt

DECORATION DAYS

This forest of flags sits atop a crowd of motor homes at a NASCAR race. Fans fly these flags to show their loyalty to drivers and to show what races they have attended in a given year.

TRACKS AND DRIVERS
T-shirts, jackets, hats, and other gear can be worn to commemorate races (the Pocono 500, above), drivers (Elliott Sadler visor, left), tracks, or just NASCAR itself.

Driver visor

Helmet mug

Fans try to get the best view of the track

Fans sit on top of the mobile homes to watch the race.

Race day

A NASCAR RACE DAY IS one of the most exciting afternoons in sports. But there is more to the day than just the race. Numerous ceremonies, qualifying rounds, and shorter races are held all weekend long to set the stage and get the fans revved up for the main event on Sunday. On the big day itself, a loud, colorful, joyous crowd fills the stands ready to cheer. The day usually kicks off with introductions of the drivers, presentation of the colors, the National Anthem, and ceremonies unique to each track. Live music from marching bands or the latest music stars pumps up the crowd. Then, as the excitement reaches fever pitch…it's time to race!

TIME TO SING
Local and national singing stars appear at NASCAR events to lead the crowd in the singing of the National Anthem before every race. Here is Miss America, Dierdre Downs, singing before the 2004 MBNA 400.

Luxury suites and press seating are on this level.

FLYOVER FESTIVITIES
A special highlight of some NASCAR events is a flyover by military jets. Roaring overhead, their engines are nearly as loud as the 43 cars!

Flag of a Texas unit

Flag representing a local community

Flags of the United States and its military units are represented by these soldiers.

SALUTING AMERICA
Local representatives of U.S. military units "present the colors" before every NASCAR race. Fans stand as the American and other flags are marched out onto the track.

Color guard weapons are not loaded.

Volunteers help spread out the flags on the infield.

NASCAR "ROCKS"

NASCAR races are very popular with celebrities from every area of entertainment. It's not unusual to see movie stars, singers, politicians, and stars from other sports in the garage areas before races. Sometimes they make the pre-race announcement of "Start your engines!" Here, actor and professional wrestler "The Rock" (center) meets with team owner Ray Evernham and driver Kasey Kahne (right) before making that call in 2004.

GETTING WARMED UP

After the flyover is finished, the flags are furled, the songs are sung, and the celebrities have headed to their seats, it's time to start the race. In this race, the pace car (in this case, a pace truck) leads the cars three times around the track. This helps drivers warm up their engines and tires, while also making sure that all 43 cars are operating properly. Then the pace car peels off the track, the green flag drops, and the race is on!

These seats near the start-finish line are some of the most sought after at the stadium.

Special box-seats section

Flag is laid out at start-finish line.

AN AMERICAN SPECTACLE

Many NASCAR events kick off with spectacular pageantry, such as this massive American flag display before the 2004 Daytona 500. Other races feature pre-race shows that include music, bands, and parades.

Pit crew

NASCAR RACING IS MUCH MORE than one man in a car—it's a team sport. Key members of that team are the pit crew, led by the crew chief. A pit crew takes care of a team's car before, during, and after a race. Before a race, pit crew members prepare the car, put on the right tires, and make sure it's fueled up for the start. During the race, they change tires, add fuel, clean the windshield, and make repairs in lightning-fast "pit stops." A team's speed during pit stops can sometimes mean the difference between winning—and finishing anywhere but first!

PIT CREW HELMET
Like drivers, NASCAR pit crew members all wear helmets made of high-impact plastic and lined with thick foam padding.

Fuelers' helmets have face guards.

HELPING HANDS
Yanking a heavy tire off a race car and putting another one on is hard on the hands. To protect their hands from the heavy equipment, tire changers wear these padded "wrenchers' gloves." Silicone fingertips make grabbing lug nuts easier.

ROLLING INTO PLACE
NASCAR vehicles are designed to go fast—not to move slowly. So before a race, the crew works together to guide the car into position in the garage or on the track by pushing it. This also helps save wear and tear on the car so that it is in peak shape for the race.

Padded palm

Silicone fingertips

Jack man uses special tool to lift one side of the car off the ground.

Treads on shoes help prevent slips.

Specially treated apron resists splashes of fuel.

SPECIAL PIT SHOES
Like most athletes, pit crew members wear shoes designed to make their job easier. The soles of these leather shoes are made to be oil resistant to help prevent slipping during hectic pit stops.

FUELERS' APRON
One of the members of the pit crew is called the "gas-can man." His job is to tip the heavy, 11-gallon (41.6-liter) fuel cans upward to fill the cars with gas during pit stops. His fire-resistant apron, treated with special chemicals, helps protect him from fuel spills.

One crew member steers the car from outside during the push to the starting grid.

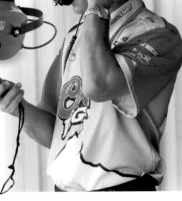

Thick rubber cups act as noise protection.

Headphone connection jack

COMMUNICATION

Crew chiefs (right), drivers, and crew members away from the track speak during the races on a radio system. Headphones like these are connected to receivers. Each team is assigned its own radio frequency.

MAN IN CHARGE

On and off the track, the crew chief is in charge of the pit crew. Crew chiefs, such as Lee McCall of Sterling Marlin's team, (above) work closely with drivers, crew members, and spotters to help cars and drivers run the best race possible. A crew chief makes split-second decisions that can impact the entire race.

CATCH AS CATCH CAN

The "catch-can man" is another member of the fueling team during pit stops. He uses this red device to catch any fuel that spills as the gas-can man pours it into the car. This key safety step helps prevent fires or dangerous spills.

FIFTEEN SECONDS MAKE THE DIFFERENCE

Several times during each race, NASCAR drivers steer their cars onto pit road. Stopping precisely in their predetermined spot, they watch as the seven-man pit crew goes "over the wall." The jack man lifts up one side of the car; the tire changers use air guns to loosen lug nuts and remove two tires. Tire carriers "hang" new tires, which are then tightened on. In the rear, the fuel team fills the tank. All this action can take less than 15 seconds! When the crew is done, the driver roars back onto the track.

Tire changers use special tools powered by long air hoses to remove and then replace tires.

The metal fuel can is hoisted into position by the gas-can man.

Tire carriers lug 80-lb (36-kg) tires into position for tire changers.

Richard Petty

By ALMOST ANY MEASURE, Richard Petty is the most successful driver in NASCAR history. In his sterling 35-year career (1958–1992) he won an astounding 200 races, almost twice as many as any other driver. He won seven NASCAR NEXTEL Cup Series championships (1964, '67, '71, '72, '74, '75, and '79), a feat matched only by Dale Earnhardt; he earned the most pole positions (127); and started the most races (1,177). He was also a seven-time winner of the Daytona 500, NASCAR's most prestigious race. In 1967, he had perhaps the greatest single season in motor sports history. He won 27 races, including 10 in a row, and finished in the top five in 38 out of 45 races. All these feats and more have truly made him "The King."

BRIGHT SMILE—BRIGHT FUTURE
Young Richard Petty had been around cars, engines, and stock-car racing all of his life, following his famous dad Lee, a three-time NASCAR NEXTEL Cup champ, around the fledgling NASCAR series. In 1959, he got his chance to join his dad in the big-time.

The King and his cars

Richard Petty has driven just about every model of stock car used in NASCAR for the past 50 years. As he moved forward in his career, he used different car models, taking advantage not only of sponsors interested in working with him, but also of technology that made engines bigger and car designs more aerodynamic. Petty's continued success proved the old NASCAR saying: It's not the car, it's the driver.

PETTY IN 1961
Richard drove this Plymouth model car in his second NASCAR season.

PETTY IN 1966
Continuing his long relationship with Plymouth, Petty finished third overall in this model. He also drove a Plymouth in his magical 1967 season, the most successful by a driver in history.

Trophy for winning the race at Talladega Superspeedway

Sponsor logos

Sloping back window

PETTY IN 1969
Petty spent only one season in this Ford Torino, a more streamlined car that helped him reach second place in the season standings with 31 top-five finishes. The numbers on the hood show the enormous size of the engine—427 cubic inches (6,997 cubic cm).

Horizontal wing

PETTY TAKES WING
In 1970, Petty and Plymouth put together this unique Road Runner car that sported a horizontal "wing" above the rear trunk area. The wing was meant to improve aerodynamic performance.

This is a toy of Petty's car.

THE KING'S LAST RIDE
As his NASCAR driving career came to a close, Petty drove this Pontiac Grand Prix through 1992. The familiar red-and-white STP paint scheme was a part of his racing team's colors starting in 1972. Petty took the number 43 to honor his father, Lee, who had driven No. 42.

FAMILIAR GROUND
Richard Petty was joined by his wife Lynda in Victory Lane after a big win in 1983.

Petty's cowboy
hat and dark
glasses became
one of his
trademarks.

**FAREWELL
TO THE KING**
Petty announced
that 1992 would be
his last season behind
the wheel. Throughout
the year, at every race,
fans turned out to honor
"The King" on his
farewell tour. Ironically,
he crashed in his final
race, but fans remember
his successes, not that
unfortunate end.

KING OF CEREAL
Richard Petty's face
has graced just about
every kind of
souvenir you can
imagine. He was on
this box of cereal after
his racing team
gained Cheerios as a
sponsor in 1998. Since
retiring from racing,
Petty has remained
very active in the
sport as a team owner
(his Petty Enterprises
No. 43 car is above),
helping young drivers
learn the lessons that
made him the best.

Cheerios
WHOLE GRAIN
General Mills
Cheerios®
Toasted Whole Grain Oat Cereal
THE NEW TEAM
Petty Enterprises & Cheerios
Red Lobster
43
NET WT 15 OZ (425g)
COLLECTOR'S EDITION

Team owner
Richard Petty
posed on this
cereal box with
his team's car.

Medal of
Freedom

Actor Paul Newman
helped Kyle start
the Camp.

DRIVING FOR DAD—AND KIDS
Kyle Petty (left) joined his famous
dad (right) on the NASCAR
circuit in 1979 and started
racing for the Petty Enterprises
team in 1992. One of the most
important lessons Kyle
learned was about
helping others. Kyle
has twice been named
NASCAR's Man of the
Year for his community
efforts, notably his
Victory Junction
Junction Gang camp for
seriously ill children.

Petty wore his cowboy hat in place
of a helmet for this ceremonial lap.

A KING AND A FIRST LADY
For his outstanding racing achievements and
his many efforts to help the community, Petty
received the Presidential Medal of Freedom,
America's highest civilian award. First Lady
Barbara Bush hung the medal around Petty's
neck during a 1992 ceremony at the White
House. Only about 400 people in history have
ever received this high honor, and Petty was
the first motorsports athlete so honored.

STILL OUT IN FRONT
While continuing his role as a team owner and advisor to
several drivers, Richard Petty got another taste of the track after
this 2003 race in Miami. Matt Kenseth, celebrating the season
championship he had won, followed Petty in his yellow DeWalt
Ford on a ceremonial victory lap. Petty drove a replica of his 1970
winged car. Ceremonies like this one link the generations of NASCAR
fans. If Kenseth can win six more times, he will catch up to The King!

Dale Earnhardt

HAPPY DALE
He earned nickname "the Intimidator" for his fierce driving style, but in this official NASCAR portrait, Dale Earnhardt took off the dark glasses and put on a winning smile.

Perhaps no other NASCAR driver has combined national popularity with record-setting success as much as Dale Earnhardt. For more than 20 years, he was at or near the top of the NASCAR ranks, winning a record-tying seven championships. Along the way, he earned a reputation as one of the toughest, most determined drivers ever. The son of NASCAR pioneer Ralph Earnhardt, Dale was the father of current star Dale Jr. and Kerry, who has raced in several series. Tragically, the great career of this NASCAR legend ended in 2001 when he died after a crash.

Earnhardt raced with the No. 19 car just once.

SECOND YEAR
This is a toy model of the car that Dale Earnhardt drove in a 1977 race in NASCAR's top series. He entered his first top-series race in 1975 and competed in both of NASCAR's top two series off and on until he joined the top ranks full-time in 1979. Earnhardt had an advantage meeting car owners thanks to his dad, Ralph, who was a former driver, but Earnhardt had to earn his own place on the track.

Earnhardt's No. 3 is as legendary as the driver himself.

Earnhardt's signature

DRIVEN TO HIS FIRST TITLE
Earnhardt joined NASCAR's top series full-time in 1979. Driving this No. 3 Wrangler car, he won one race, had 11 top-five finishes, and was named rookie of the year. In 1980, he became the first driver to follow that award with a NASCAR championship. That year he had five wins and 19 top-fives.

"THE MAN IN BLACK"
In 1981, Earnhardt joined the racing team owned by former driver Richard Childress. He began driving this black No. 3 Goodwrench car, earning him his famous nickname, "the Man in Black." He won championships again in 1986, 1987, 1990, 1991, 1993, and 1994. In 1998, after 19 unsuccessful attempts, he won his first and only Daytona 500 race.

Checkered flag pattern mimics the flag used at end of NASCAR races.

FATHER AND SON
In 1998, Dale Sr. welcomed Dale Jr. to the top racing ranks. That year, both were chosen to join drivers from a variety of racing styles in the International Race of Champions in Daytona, in which all competitors drove identically prepared cars. Victory went to Dale Sr.

OP OF THE ACING WORLD
arnhardt stopped affic in New York's mes Square in 94 when he went town to claim his venth NASCAR EXTEL Cup ampionship ophy, only the cond driver ever reach that total.

Earnhardt mania

A combination of driving skills and a no-nonsense personality made Dale Earnhardt a racing legend. He inspired thousands of different types of souvenirs and memorabilia, from traditional trading cards to jewelry.

No. 3 represents Earnhardt's car number.

FUN FOR THE FANS
Dale Earnhardt earned the respect of NASCAR fans of all ages (and both sexes). This souvenir charm bracelet features checkered flags, Earnhardt's car number, and his familiar black car. Even after his death, Earnhardt remains a fan favorite.

"The Intimidator" poses

TRADING CARDS
Like any sports hero, Dale Earnhardt inspired numerous trading cards. These are just two examples. On the upper card, he strikes a familiar pose. He won a total of 76 races in his 22-year career.

Souvenir trading card

DEVOTED TO DALE
NASCAR fans are known for their loyalty, and no driver commanded as much loyalty as Earnhardt. Here, Oklahoma fan Mike Miller shows off his "shrine" to his favorite driver, which features hundreds of souvenirs, cards, posters, and other pieces of memorabilia.

Jeff Gordon

After Richard Petty and Dale Earnhardt, Jeff Gordon is the most successful driver ever in terms of winning NASCAR NEXTEL Cup titles. In 1992, he made his debut, fittingly, in the last race run by Richard Petty. Gordon zoomed upward and won his first title in 1995. He won the championship three more times before he turned 31.

FAMILIAR SIGHT
Gordon's brightly colored No. 24 car, sponsored by a paint company, can often be seen near the lead.

PORTABLE GORDON
You know that an athlete has made it big when he has an action figure modeled after him. This figure was first sold in 2003.

The brick topping this trophy is a symbol of the Brickyard track.

FAST STARTER
In 1977, Simpson Racing Products made its smallest racing suit ever for Jeff, then six years old, and racing in his native California (left). In 1992, the go-kart star won his first race in NASCAR, commemorated on the card at right.

HIS SECOND HOME
Jeff Gordon moved to racing-crazy Indiana as a young child. In 1994 (left), he went back to Indiana to win the first Brickyard 400, a NASCAR race held at the famous Indianapolis Motor Speedway.

A BIG WIN IN CALIFORNIA
Through 2004, Jeff has crossed the finish line 69 times in only 12 full seasons, an average of nearly six wins per year. This win in 2004 (right) came at the California Speedway, a newer venue that is now home to two NASCAR races each season. The victory also gave Jeff a checkered flag in his home state for the fourth time, including two road-course wins at the twisty Infineon Raceway north of San Francisco.

More NASCAR stars

The cars are impressive, but the drivers behind the wheel are the real stars of NASCAR. These drivers become stars for their on-track success, their driving styles and techniques, and their trips to Victory Lane, but they also become popular thanks to their manners off the track. The drivers pictured here and on the next pages are among the top stars of NASCAR. Some of these drivers may one day become NASCAR legends.

Visor is tinted to cut glare.

EARLY WINNER
Kurt Busch only started racing full time on the NASCAR NEXTEL Cup Series in 2001, but he has quickly made an impact. In 2004, he won the closest season championship race in NASCAR history, winning by eight points.

NEXT BROTHER UP
Kurt Busch's younger brother Kyle, after a successful career in NASCAR's number-two series, joined his big brother in the top series in 2005. Though Kyle gets attention for his family connections, he's got the talent to shine on his own.

SUPERSTAR ON AND OFF THE TRACK
Blessed with loads of racing talent and one of the most famous names in NASCAR, Dale Earnhardt Jr. (left) has become one of the sport's most popular personalities. Along with making appearances in Victory Lane, he can be seen all over the media; here he is on *Live with Regis and Kelly*, a national talk show.

"HAPPY" TO BE HERE
His off-track nickname might be "Happy," but Kevin Harvick has made a lot of other drivers unhappy with his success in recent seasons. He won four races in his first four full NASCAR NEXTEL Cup seasons, including the Brickyard 400 in 2003.

COLORFUL STAR
Elliott Sadler has been an up-and-coming star since his NASCAR debut in 1998. After six good seasons, he broke out in 2004, finishing in the top 10 to take part in the first Chase for the NASCAR NEXTEL Cup. Driving his candy-colored No. 38 car, he finished the season ninth, with bright hopes for more "sweet" seasons ahead.

Transponder sends information from car to race teams and TV crews.

Both cars benefit from reduced drag in Newman's wake.

WIMMER A FUTURE WINNER?
Scott Wimmer (in his no. 22 car, above) was only a rookie in 2004, but he made a solid first impression with a third-place finish in the season-opening Daytona 500. Scott wound up 27th overall at season's end, but look for big things in his future.

A FAVORITE MARTIN
Mark Martin (facing front) has been near the top of the NASCAR charts since his second full-time season in 1988. From 1989 through 2000, he was in the top 10 at the end of the season. He joined the group of "young guns" in the 2004 Chase for the NASCAR NEXTEL Cup, finishing in fourth place.

ENGINEERING A VICTORY
Ryan Newman is shown here leading a three-car draft with Brian Vickers and Jimmie Johnson. (When drafting, cars follow another car very closely, cutting the air resistance they have to battle against.) Along with being an ace driver, Newman holds an engineering degree from Purdue University. He often uses his technical expertise to help his team improve his car.

FAST TO THE FUTURE
Brian Vickers is one of a number of drivers who are starting to make their mark. In 2004, his rookie season, Vickers (in his No. 25 car) was 25th overall, but he was often in contention for the lead.

THREE FOR THE ROAD
This trio of drivers includes a NASCAR legend, a former champ, and a driver many peg as a future champ. No. 24 is Jeff Gordon, the four-time champ. No. 17 is 2003 winner Matt Kenseth. No. 9 is Kasey Kahne, the top-finishing rookie during the 2004 season.

BREAKOUT SEASON
Jeremy Mayfield broke out in a big way in 2004. With one win and 13 top-10 finishes, he earned a spot in the Top 10 for the Chase for the NASCAR NEXTEL Cup.

A STAR MEETS THE FANS
These NASCAR fans know a star when they see one, and they are crowding behind this pit-area wall to meet Jimmie Johnson. Through 2005, Jimmie had raced full-time on NASCAR's top level for only three seasons, but had finished fifth, second, and second, marking him a driver to watch.

HERE'S TO A CHAMP
In 2003, only his fourth full-time season of NASCAR NEXTEL Cup racing, Matt Kenseth stood atop the charts at the end of the year. He put together a remarkably consistent season, with 25 top-10 finishes, to capture the championship.

Manhattan's famous Times Square

Fans in New York's Times Square crowded around Matt and his car when he was in town to accept his championship trophy.

NASCAR families

FATHERS, SONS, BROTHERS, AND MORE—when racing is in a family's blood, it tends to carry on through the generations. Since its founding, NASCAR has been led by the France family. They have watched a large number of other families send multiple members into the larger NASCAR family, some of them among the most successful drivers ever. Other family members have contributed behind the scenes as builders, managers, or just by being there when family is needed.

THE FAMILY FLOCK
Among the earliest stars were the Flock family, led by Tim, above, who won top honors in 1952 and 1955. Tim, who finished his career with 40 race victories in only 189 starts, sometimes drove with a monkey in the car!

ANOTHER FROM THE FLOCK
Truman Fontello "Fonty" Flock seemed to specialize in coming in second. Along with being the second-oldest in the family, he recorded 20 runner-up finishes in his career (and 19 wins). Brother Bob and sister Ethel also raced, the only time in NASCAR history that four siblings have raced.

NASCAR first family

The France family's vision and leadership built NASCAR and helped it grow to become the nation's most popular motor sport. Bill France, Sr., got it all started in 1947, and his son and grandson have kept the sport zooming ahead at top speed for more than 50 years. The France family history of breaking away from racing traditions has helped make NASCAR even more exciting—and popular.

Trophy to honor France's work

THE FIRST FRANCE
The father of NASCAR, Bill France, Sr., was also the father of a key NASCAR family who has kept his vision alive. A former auto mechanic and race car driver turned racing promoter and entrepreneur, "Big Bill" made sure to keep NASCAR " all in the family," assuring its success.

THE SECOND FRANCE
Bill France, Jr. (right) took over for his dad, Bill, Sr. (left) in 1972 after learning the ropes of the family business. Bill, Jr. oversaw enormous growth in the sport's national popularity and television audience.

TODAY'S FRANCE
In 2003, Brian France, th grandson of Bill France Sr., and son of Bill Franc Jr., took over as presiden of NASCAR, continuin a family legacy that stretched from the day of racing on the sands

Terry accepts a trophy for winning the 2003 Mountain Dew 400.

MOM WOULD BE PROUD
Terry Labonte (left) is six years older than his brother Bobby, so it's only fair that he got the first NASCAR NEXTEL Cup Series title in the family. But Bobby matched him in 2000, and the brothers set a new standard for sibling rivalry. On the track, they try to beat each other; off the track, they're each others' biggest fans. The two are the only brothers to both win the championship of NASCAR's top series.

Portraits of Dale, Jr., and Dale, Sr., painted on bottle.

Palm trees on trophy represent South Carolina, the site of the race.

...D SHOWING HIS BOYS THE ROPES
...ood was thicker than gasoline in the ...rth Carolina garage of the Petty ...mily. Patriarch Lee (center) was ...e of NASCAR's first top drivers, ...nning three series championships ... well as the first Daytona 500 in ...59. Maurice Petty (left) was an ace ...gine builder and key part of the ...m that helped brother Richard ...ght) win a record 200 races in his ...azing racing career.

BIG TIRE TRACKS TO FOLLOW
Dale Earnhardt, Jr. has the most famous name in racing, thanks to his dad Dale, Sr.'s seven championships and unmatched reputation for toughness and desire. This soda bottle, issued in 2000, celebrates their first full season racing together in 1999.

SEE YOU ON THE TRUCK, DAD
Jimmie Johnson is one of today's best young drivers, twice finishing second overall in NASCAR NEXTEL Cup Series season standings. But he depends on an older driver to get him where he's going. Jimmie's dad Greg drives his son's team's transport truck from racetrack to racetrack.

Both Kenny and Rusty drove Dodges in 2004.

The Jarretts posed before the 1998 Brickyard 400, just before Ned interviewed Dale on TV.

LIKE FATHER, LIKE SON
Ned Jarrett was one of the top drivers in NASCAR in the late 1950s and early 1960s. The short-track ace was the top series champion in 1961 and 1965, and won 50 career races. After retirement, he became one of the most well-known TV announcers in NASCAR. His son Dale is also a racing ace, winning the NASCAR NEXTEL CUP championship in 1999, three Daytona 500s, and 31 career races.

...EATING HIS BROTHER
...he Wallace brothers are a fast-moving family. Pictured here ...Kenny Wallace (front) passing his older brother Rusty during ...2003 race. Rusty was the 1989 NASCAR NEXTEL Cup ...ampion and has won 55 races. Kenny had his first full season ...the top series in 1993. A third Wallace brother, Mike, races ...the NASCAR Craftsman Truck Series.

NASCAR's No. 2 Series

A SET OF CHAMPS
This special print features personally autographed postcards of former champions of this number-two series. Jack Ingram was a five-time champ in the 1970s and 1980s. Sam Ard won it all in 1983–84. Tommy Houston was runner-up in 1989. Randy LaJoie was tops in 1996–97.

Since 1982, NASCAR's number two series has existed in the form it takes today: drivers in cars slightly less powerful than NASCAR NEXTEL Cup cars race on many of the same tracks, in shorter races, on Saturday—the day before NASCAR NEXTEL Cup races. But the action is just as furious and intense as Sunday's races. Some drivers are hoping to succeed here and move up to the next level. Other drivers compete in both series, racing back-to-back on Saturdays and Sundays.

PAINTING A WINNER
Race winners take home unique trophies for winning. This trophy featuring a billboard design goes to winners of a race in Nazareth, Pennsylvania.

Air scoops help keep the car aerodynamic.

OPPORTUNITY KNOCKED
Not many women have earned rides in NASCAR stock cars, but one who has is Tina Gordon, who started 12 races in the number-two series in 2004 and won more than $200,000.

SIMILAR BUT SLOWER
Cars in the number-two series (like this #9 car) have basically the same construction as those in the NASCAR NEXTEL Cup series, but they are slightly longer and wider (by a matter of inches), with less powerful engines (660 vs. 790 horsepower).

WORKING UP THE LADDER
Casey Mears is a good example of a driver who has worked his way up the NASCAR ladder. He joined the number-two series in 2002, where he finished 21st. Team owner Chip Ganassi saw Mears' talent and promoted him to the NASCAR NEXTEL Cup Series in 2003, and he finished 35th. By 2004, he had moved up to 22nd and won two poles.

Crew members wear uniforms with sponsor logos, too.

KEEP 'EM RUNNIN' Some race teams run cars in both of the top two series. Most operate with a separate crews for each car, but some specialists, such as mechanics, double up and work on both.

EY, ISN'T THAT…?
's not unusual to see top NASCAR EXTEL Cup drivers take part in vo races in one weekend. Matt enseth was the 2003 NASCAR EXTEL Cup champion, but he oves racing and winning so much at he also drives in second-series vents. Here he poses with the rophy he won at the 2004 O'Reilly 0 race at Texas.

Drivers' uniforms in this series are also covered with sponsor colors and logos.

ITS A TEAM GAME
Another example of the crossover between NASCAR's two top series is race teams. Here owner Richard Childress, long a force at the Nextel Cup level, holds his 2003 owners' championship trophy, thanks to drivers Johnny Sauter and Kevin Harvick, the latter a top driver in Nextel Cup.

LOOK FAMILIAR?
ohnny Sauter (27), Derrick Cope (49), and Greg Biffle (60) roar around a curve during he 2004 MBNA America 200-mile (320 m) race at Dover International Raceway. In comparison, the NASCAR NEXTEL Cup race the ext day on the same track was 400 miles 644 km) long.

The second-series cars are 3 inches (7.6 cm) wider and 2 inches (5 cm) longer than NASCAR NEXTEL Cup race cars.

Checkered flag

TAKING THE CHECKER
Victory is sweet in any motor sports race. Here's Jamie McMurray winning in North Carolina in 2004, sweeping under the checkered flag.

NASCAR Craftsman Truck Series

NASCAR RACING IS NOT just for cars. The NASCAR Craftsman Truck Series, which began in 1995, features specially modified pickup trucks. The series races on many of the same oval tracks used by cars in NASCAR's other top series. The first NASCAR truck race was held in 1995, at Phoenix International Raceway. Since then, the series has expanded to include about 25 events per year. One unique aspect of truck racing is the presence of Toyota; it's the only NASCAR series in which the Japanese carmaker has vehicles.

SPEEDY TRUCKER
Jack Sprague is the only driver to win three season championships in the NASCAR Craftsman Truck Series, in 1997, 1999, and 2001. He has won more prize money than any other truck racer.

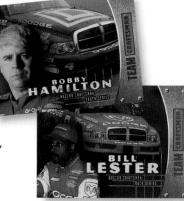

TRUCK SOUVENIRS
Fans of the NASCAR Craftsman Truck Series can collect trading cards of their favorite drivers, such as Bobby Hamilton or Bill Lester, shown here.

This is not a real check that can be cashed at a bank.

Like car racers, truck drivers sport colorful racing uniforms covered with sponsor logos.

WOMAN BEHIND THE WHEEL
The NASCAR Craftsman Truck Series has featured several female drivers. Tina Gordon, who took part in 11 races in 2003, also has raced in the series below the NNCS.

THE KID AND THE VET
Chad Chaffin (left) had a lot of success in NASCAR's second-highest series before moving to trucks in 2003. He notched his first two race wins in 2003 and finished in the top 10 in 2003 and 2004. Bobby Hamilton, on the other hand, has been around the track a few times. In 2004, at the age of 47, he became the oldest champion in the NASCAR Crasftsman Truck series history.

Truck beds are enclosed for less air resistance.

Headlight stickers

NASCAR trucks' engines are slightly smaller and less powerful than stock car engines.

TRUCK SMACK!
Moving at more than 150 miles per hour, just a bit slower than their car counterparts, vehicles in the NASCAR Craftsman Truck Series can end up in slam-bang action, too, as in this 2004 race.

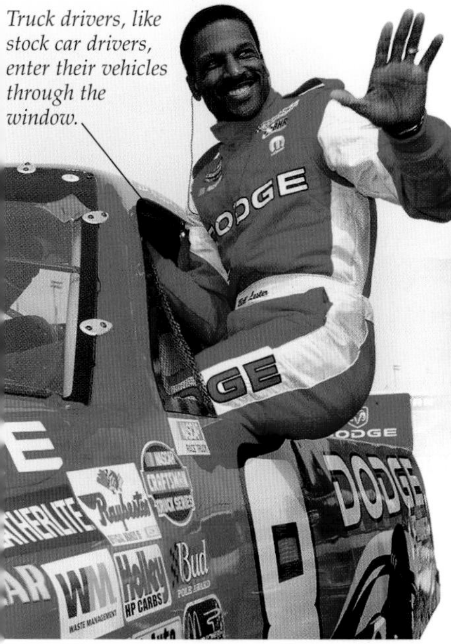

Truck drivers, like stock car drivers, enter their vehicles through the window.

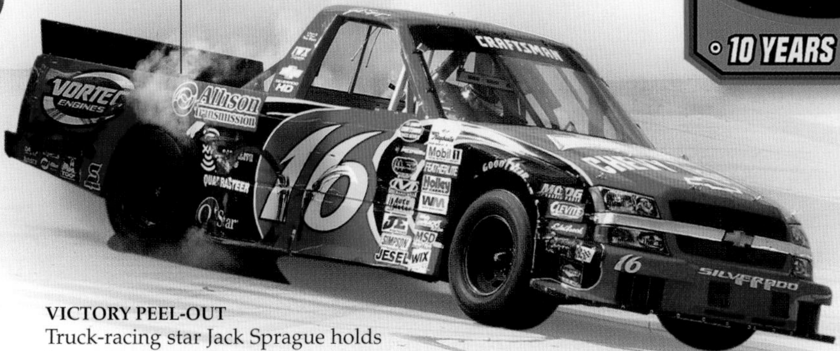

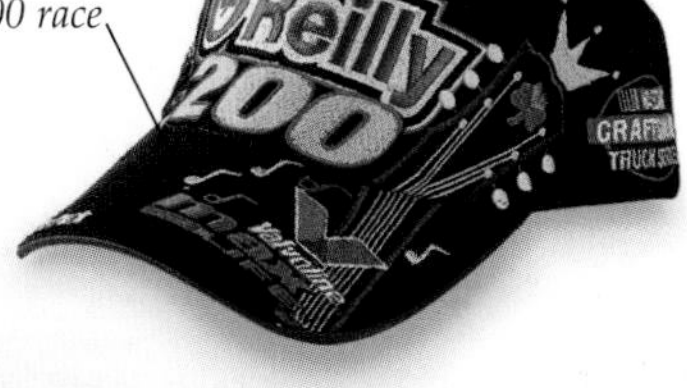

LESTER AT WORK
Bill Lester is one of the most prominent African-American drivers in the NASCAR family of racing series. The 2004 season was his third driving in the NASCAR Craftsman Truck Series.

1995 – 2005
NASCAR
CRAFTSMAN
TRUCK SERIES
10 YEARS TOUGH

HAPPY ANNIVERSARY!
This new logo design marks 10 years of action in the fast-growing, fast-paced NASCAR Craftsman Truck Series.

Tires smoke as they spin.

VICTORY PEEL-OUT
Truck-racing star Jack Sprague holds the series records for top-five and top-10 finishes. Here he is spinning out his tires after winning a race during the 2004 season.

Skidmarks left by the truck's spinout

Cap from O'Reilly 200 race

RACING "LID"
Fans of truck racing have souvenirs just like those in the car series. This cap is from a 2004 race.

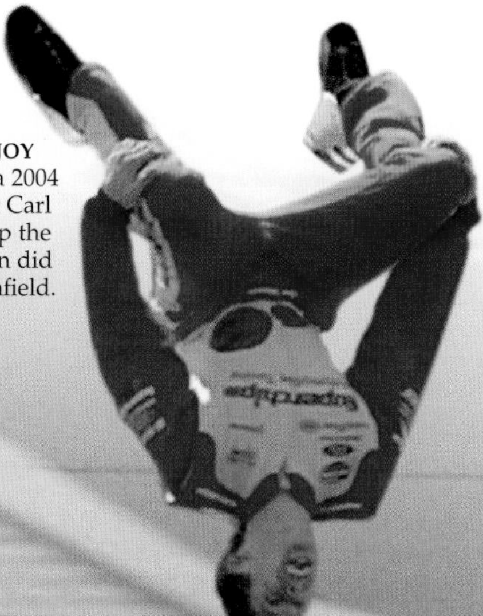

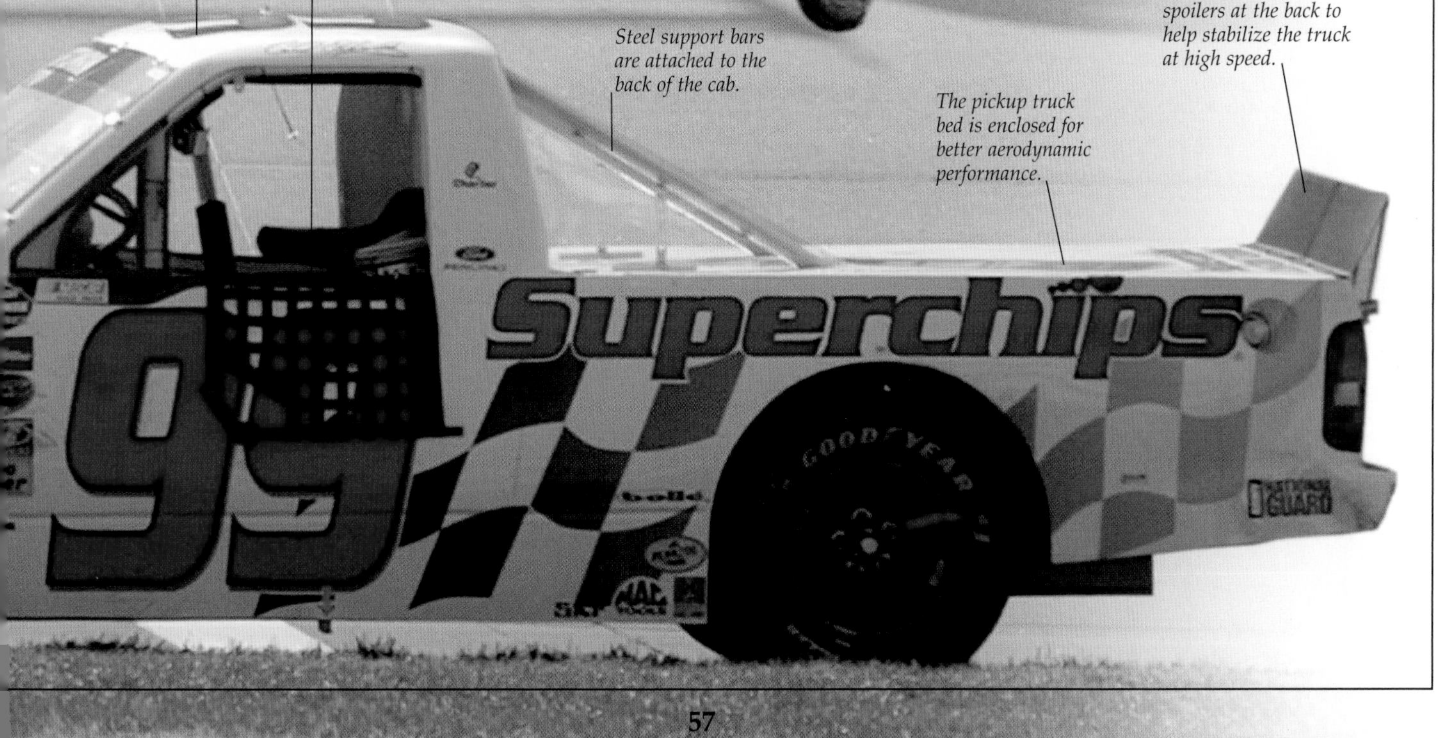

JUMP FOR JOY
To celebrate winning a 2004 race at Daytona, driver Carl Edwards climbed atop the bed of his truck and then did a backflip onto the infield.

Racing trucks are about eight inches (20 cm) higher than stock cars.

Nylon netting covers window opening.

Steel support bars are attached to the back of the cab.

The pickup truck bed is enclosed for better aerodynamic performance.

Like stock cars, racing trucks have adjustable spoilers at the back to help stabilize the truck at high speed.

Back straightaway is
3,400 ft (1,036 m) long

Pit road

Start/finish line

THE SPEEDWAY
This track map of Daytona
International Speedway, which
opened in 1959, shows the
distinctive D-shape, called a
"tri-oval" by NASCAR drivers.

Daytona 500

NASCAR'S MOST IMPORTANT RACE is also the first major race on its calendar every year. Since its first running in 1959, the Daytona 500 has become perhaps America's most famous and beloved motor race. Held at Florida's Daytona International Speedway each February, "the 500" is a top career goal for any stock-car racer, second only to winning the NASCAR championship itself. All of NASCAR's greatest drivers have succeeded on Daytona's high-banked tri-oval track, and many of the all-time highlights in stock-car racing have taken place there.

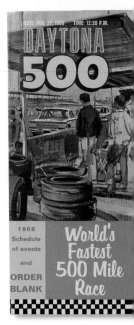

SIGN UP HERE
Fans who wanted to come to Daytona to watch the 500 in 1968 used this ticket order form. Spectators at that year's race saw Cale Yarborough win the first of his three career 500s.

TICKET TO RIDE
This is a ticket to the first Daytona 500 on February 22, 1959. The Ralph DePalma grandstand was named after a former Indy 500 winner.

SPEED THRILLS
This program was sold at the 1969 Daytona 500. It features the then-famous powder-blue No. 43 car driven by Richard Petty.

**THE FIRST FINISH,
FAST AND FURIOUS**
The first running of the Daytona 500 was one of the most thrilling races ever. Johnny Beauchamp (73) and Lee Petty (42), a three-time NASCAR champ and father of future seven-time champ Richard Petty, were neck-and-neck heading toward the finish line. The two crossed the finish line in a near dead-heat. Beauchamp was declared the winner, but the decision was given to Petty three days later after race officials studied newsreel footage of the finish.

Fans in Daytona's lower grandstand are close to the action.

THREE OUT OF SEVEN
After his father Lee paved the way, Richard Petty became the greatest driver in the history of NASCAR's biggest race. Here he is in 1971 taking the checkered flag to win the third of his record seven career Daytona 500 victories.

Car numbers on roof can be read when cars go around banked turns.

THERE HE GOES AGAIN

After 1972, Richard Petty drove the red-and-blue STP car that would become his lasting trademark. Here, he is shown in the 1973 Daytona 500, zooming around the No. 8 car driven by Ed Negre. Petty passed everyone else by the end and won his fourth Daytona 500.

"426 C.I." refers to the car's 426 cubic-inch engine.

HISTORICAL EVENT

This is a ticket for the 1998 Daytona 500, the 40th in the series and one of the most memorable for race fans. NASCAR was celebrating its 50th anniversary, and Dale Earnhardt had something to celebrate as well—he won the race for the first time.

Ticket features photos of Daytona's famous main grandstand.

HIS GUY WON?

In one of the most dramatic moments in NASCAR history, all-time legends Richard Petty and David Pearson dueled fender to fender on the last lap of the 1976 Daytona 500. Nearing the end, they suddenly crashed, and both cars spun into the infield. Although his car ended up taking quite a beating, Pearson coaxed it past the finish line moments later to capture the victory.

GORDON GOES TO THE FRONT

Jeff Gordon (front right) holds the pole position at the 1999 Daytona 500. Gordon went on to win this race, his second career victory in NASCAR's big event.

Trophy features model of early "speed" car driven on Daytona Beach sands.

A SECOND-GENERATION WINNER

In 2004, Dale Earnhardt Jr. claimed this Daytona 500 trophy. Unlike his famous father, he won the race just four years into his top-series career.

NASCAR on TV

Since 1989, every NASCAR race has been shown on national television. This has opened up the excitement of stock car racing to millions of fans. Not only are the races broadcast live across the U.S., but fans can watch the nail-biting drama of qualifying rounds (where drivers take laps to determine starting positon), and go behind the scenes with lifestyle shows like NASCAR 360. Cable stations such as SPEED Channel provide hours of NASCAR-related programming each week, including high-definition broadcasts. Special cable options let viewers listen in to team radio broadcasts during races. Here's a look at the technology that brings NASCAR to your television screen.

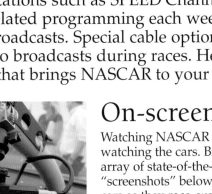

Dashboard driver camera

On-screen graphics

Watching NASCAR on TV means more than just watching the cars. Broadcasters also offer a wide array of state-of-the-art on-screen graphics. The "screenshots" below show how viewers can track cars as they race, watch throttle and brake usage, find out how fast cars are moving, and keep constant tabs on the order of the cars.

IN THE PITS
During a race, reporters are on the spot in the pit and garage areas to get the latest news on cars, engines, crews, and drivers. Coordinating it all is an announcer on the NBC network "war wagon," which is a large metal box with seats for announcers and places for monitors, cameras, and wires. Manning the desk here is NBC Sports' Bill Weber.

Roll cage "look ahead" camera

GETTING THE PICTURE
Tiny cameras (black tubes) are mounted on the roll cage above the car's dashboard or behind the driver. When activated, the cameras give viewers an incredible view of the intense action inside the car or a view of the track from the driver's perspective.

THE CONTROL TRUCK
This is the TV control truck at a NASCAR race. The director (center) examines feed from dozens of cameras to select which shots of the track will be seen by the viewers.

Monitors are labeled by camera number.

Clock shows running time of broadcast.

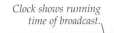

Lap number

Running order of race

Car numbers show positions on track.

GRAPHICS ADD INFORMATION
Track shots are enhanced with graphics to provide extra information. The shot at the far right includes a graphic that shows where cars are on the track; the small track shape shows the No. 9 logo chasing the No. 6 logo. The shot at the left includes a graphic that tells speed, RPMs, and levels of throttle and brake usage.

Darrell's hair and makeup people don't really wear helmets!

Headphones connect reporter to control truck.

TALK, TALK, TALK
Driver Mark Martin takes a moment after qualifying to talk with a SPEED Channel reporter. NASCAR drivers spend a lot of time talking to the media to help explain the races to their fans.

3 MINUTES TO AIR

Interview show host   Elliott Sadler   Kurt Busch   Ryan Newman

STUDIO SHOT
Television captures NASCAR drivers away from the track, too. Studio interviews like this one let fans learn more about their favorite drivers. Other shows take viewers behind the scenes of life in and around NASCAR. Many drivers also record video or audio clips that are available to fans on race team Web sites.

EXPERT VOICES
Channels that broadcast NASCAR races employ experienced pros to cover the race. Hiring a former driver to provide race coverage gives viewers an insider's perspective. One of the most successful drivers-turned-announcers is three-time NASCAR champ Darrell Waltrip. Here, he is getting ready for race day in a posed "pit crew" shot.

Dale, Jr. gets a warm hug of congratulations

CAPTURING THE MOMENT
TV cameras are joined by still photographers surrounding Dale Earnhardt, Jr. as he celebrates winning the 2004 Daytona 500. TV coverage lets fans around the world take part in these memorable moments as they happen.

Victory Lane

The NASCAR Nextel Cup

THERE'S ONLY ONE PLACE that every NASCAR driver wants to be at the end of race day: Standing up in Victory Lane to accept the winner's trophy. Located on the infield at most tracks, this special area is reserved for winners only. Right after the race, the winning driver steers his car toward this area, climbs out, and is showered with cheers and confetti (and probably some soda and champagne). After he climbs out, he raises up a trophy and creates a memory he'll take with him forever. This page shows just a few examples of the unique trophies awarded to winners of various NASCAR races.

All-Star Challenge trophy
Lowe's Motor Speedway

Sirius 400 Michigan
International Speedway

Ryan Newman shows where he finished with the familiar "I'm number one" gesture.

Drivers don baseball caps showing sponsors' names.

A WINNING PAIR
At Victory Lane, a pageant winner often posed with the driver who won the trophy. Here Johnny Beauchamp smiles after "winning" the 1959 Daytona 500. One problem: Three days later, Lee Petty was declared the real winner!

NOW THAT'S A TROPHY!
Ryan Newman poses in Victory Lane next to a one-of-a-kind trophy. The track at Dover International Speedway in Delaware is known as the "Monster Mile." Ryan won the MBNA America 400 there in 2004, and can now put this monster of a trophy on his mantelpiece at home.

BRINGING IT ALL HOME
To wrap up our tour of NASCAR, here's a photo that shows an entire winning race team—owner, driver, pit crew, garage crew, transport people, family members, and more—all surrounding the trophy they have all worked so long and hard to earn. The driver, Michael Waltrip, gets to hold it, front and center.

Fake soda inside

Abstract trophy top

Aluminum and acryclic model of track

South Carolina 200
Darlington Raceway

Coca-Cola 600
Lowe's Motor Speedway

FAMILIAR SHAPE
Winners of the Pepsi 400, the "other" famous race at Daytona International Speedway, take home this trophy that features a metal replica of the famous tri-oval Daytona track.

A WINNER ON HIS WAY
On his way to the 2004 NASCAR NEXTEL Cup championship—what you might call the ultimate Victory Lane—Kurt Busch accepted this trophy for winning the Food City 500 at Bristol Motor Speedway.

A stage is often set up in Victory Lane to hold the race team.

THE PLACE WHERE THE CAR IS A STAR
This overhead view shows how even the winning car often take center stage on Victory Lane. Here, Bill Elliott's famous number 9 car is rolled into the celebration. His crew, in red, stands with him, while dozens of camerapeople record the action. Live TV interviews are also often held in Victory Lane.

The floor of Victory Lane is often painted to match the black-and-white checkered flag waved over the race winner.

Did you know?

FASCINATING FACTS

NASCAR drivers don't worry about dirty windshields during a race. Each car's windshield is covered with up to three thin sheets of transparent plastic called "tear offs." If track debris leaves a mark on the windshield, one of the tear offs is pulled off at the next pit stop.

In 2004, 17 of the top 20 highest-attended sporting events in the United States were NASCAR races. More than 14 million people watched a NASCAR race in 2004.

Pit crews work quickly to get a car back in the race.

In March, 2005, NASCAR held a points race outside the United States for the first time in its history. Martin Truex Jr. won the Telcel Mexico 200 in Mexico City. Nearly 100,000 fans attended the race.

The last time a pair of brothers started first and second in the same race was on April 9, 2000. Rusty Wallace had the pole position, while his brother Kenny was beside him in the front row.

Since 1989, every NASCAR NEXTEL Cup race has been seen on national television. The first broadcast of a major NASCAR event occured on January 31, 1960, when CBS Sports telecast a two-hour stock-car racing special from Daytona.

Drivers aren't the only ones in a NASCAR race with super speed. The members of a team's pit crew can change a car's tires, fill its gas tank, and even clean the windshield and make repairs, all in less than 15 seconds.

Want to be a NASCAR driver? Get in shape! NASCAR drivers have to be fit and tough enough to withstand temperatures that can reach 140°F (60°C). They can lose from 5 to 10 pounds (2 to 4 kg) during the race due to the heat.

Drivers of the team haulers (the giant trucks that carry gear from track to track) each drive about 65,000 miles (104,607 km) every season. That's more than twice around the Earth from February through November!

NASCAR drivers would like to lose their marbles—the ones on the track, that is. Bits of rubber that fly off tires and debris blown onto the track are nicknamed "marbles." Speeding over marbles can cause the driver to lose control.

In 1978, President Jimmy Carter, a native of NASCAR-crazy Georgia, invited several top NASCAR drivers and officials to the White House, a first-time honor for the sport.

Lee Petty was declared the winner of the first Daytona 500 at Daytona International Speedway on February 22, 1959— but not until 61 hours after the checkered flag flew, due to a dramatic photo finish.

Early NASCAR star Tim Flock drove eight races with his monkey Jocko along for the ride. Tim once had to make a pit stop when Jocko grabbed his helmet!

After winning seven NASCAR NEXTEL Cup championships, Richard Petty knows all about speed. But he didn't go faster than the speed of sound (750 mph or 1,207 km/h) until 2001 when he hitched a ride with the U.S. Air Force's famous "Blue Angels" stunt flying team.

NASCAR NEXTEL Cup's longest race is the Coca-Cola 600 at Lowe's Motor Speedway in Charlotte, North Carolina, where drivers race for 600 miles (965 km). The shortest race distance is 218.9 miles (352 km), at Infineon Raceway in Sonoma, California.

The oldest facility on NASCAR's regular list of racetracks is Darlington Raceway in South Carolina, which has been hosting races since 1950. The newest track is the Kansas Speedway, which opened in 2001.

Three-time NASCAR NEXTEL Cup champ Lee Petty

In 1985, Bill Elliott claimed a $1 million bonus from R. J. Reynolds for winning three of the four crown jewel races on the NASCAR schedule. Elliott was victorious in the Daytona 500, the Winston 500 at Talladega, and the Southern 500 at Darlington. For this impressive accomplishment, Elliott earned the nickname "Million Dollar Bill."

Action at NASCAR's newest track, the Kansas Speedway

The green flag drops on a NASCAR starting field.

Q **How long are NASCAR tracks?**

A Superspeedways are at least a mile (1.6 km) in length and allow the fastest speeds. Short tracks are less than a mile (1.6 km) around.

Q **What car models are driven in the three national series in NASCAR?**

A Although today's stock cars are no longer taken directly from manufacturers' "stock" of passenger cars, they are still based on passenger-car types. In the NASCAR NEXTEL Cup Series and NASCAR's No. 2 series, drivers can choose from three car models: the Chevrolet Monte Carlo, the Dodge Charger, and the Ford Taurus. In the NASCAR Craftsman Truck Series, drivers have four trucks to choose from: the Chevrolet C1500 (Silverado), the Dodge Ram 1500, the Ford F-150, and the Toyota Tundra.

Q **How does a person become a NASCAR NEXTEL Cup driver?**

A For a sport that thrives on speed, it actually can be a slow process to become a driver. Like many sports, drivers work their way up through the ranks of lower divisions. There are many regional race teams where drivers get started.

Q **Who owns the cars? Do the drivers buy the cars or do the sponsors?**

A NASCAR cars are owned by racing teams, often owned or controlled by one person. These people hire drivers and get sponsors to support their teams.

Q **What is a restrictor plate? In which races is it used?**

A A restrictor plate is a thin, square piece of aluminum with four holes in it. It is placed inside an engine's carburetor to reduce airflow into the engine, and thus reduce the car's speed. NASCAR rules require the plates in races at Daytona and Talladega to ensure greater driver safety.

Q **What is the fastest racetrack in NASCAR?**

A Judging by highest average speed throughout the race, the fastest track is the Talladega Superspeedway in Talladega, Alabama, where Mark Martin averaged 188 mph (302 km/h) in a 1997 race.

Q **What is "drafting"? How do drivers use it in a race?**

A When a driver follows very closely behind another car, the second car encounters less air resistance than the first. This is known as "drafting" and allows the second car to use less fuel while going the same speed.

Q **When did NASCAR start racing specially modified pickup trucks?**

A The NASCAR Craftsman Truck Series debuted in 1995. The first race was held on February 5, 1995, at Phoenix International Raceway. There are now about 25 races on each year's schedule, including races on superspeedways and smaller tracks.

Q **What prizes does the NASCAR NEXTEL Cup champion receive?**

A The champion receives the NASCAR NEXTEL Cup trophy, along with championship bonus prize money. The total prize changes each year, but since 1972 the champion's bonus has risen from $227,015 to more than $5 million. The champion is also honored at the annual awards banquet, held in New York City in December.

Q **Who won the first NASCAR race? How much did he earn?**

A Red Byron, driving a Ford, was the winner of the first official NASCAR race, held on February 15, 1948. The course was in Daytona Beach, on both the beach sand itself and an adjoining roadway. Red went on to become NASCAR's first season champion, winning two of six races and a grand total of $5,800.

Record Breakers

NASCAR NEXTEL CUP drivers are continuing in their race for these all-time records:

- **MOST RACE WINS:**
  Richard Petty, 200

- **MOST RACE WINS (MODERN ERA, 1972 TO PRESENT):**
  Darrell Waltrip, 84

- **MOST WINNINGS IN A SINGLE SEASON:**
  Jeff Gordon, 2001: $10,879,757

- **BEST FINISH BY A FEMALE DRIVER:**
  Sara Christian, fifth place, October 2, 1949

- **OLDEST RACE WINNER:**
  Harry Gant, 52, August 16, 1992

- **YOUNGEST RACE WINNER:**
  Donald Thomas, 20, November 16, 1952

- **MOST WINS ON ONE TRACK, CAREER:**
  Richard Petty, 15, Martinsville Speedway and North Wilkesboro

- **MOST CONSECUTIVE WINS ON ROAD COURSES:**
  Jeff Gordon, 6, 1997–2000

The No. 12 car is drafting behind the No. 72 car.

Who's who?

In 1998, to celebrate NASCAR's 50th anniversary, a panel of experts chose the top 50 drivers in the history of the sport. From the earliest dirt-track daredevils to today's top superspeedway superstars, this list includes the finest stock-car drivers of all time.

BOBBY ALLISON
Alabama native Bobby Allison's 25-year NASCAR NEXTEL Cup career was highlighted by winning the 1983 series championship. He also finished second in the series five different times, while winning 84 races and three Daytona 500s.

DAVEY ALLISON
In 1987, Allison became the first NASCAR NEXTEL Cup Series rookie to qualify on the front row for a Daytona 500.

BUCK BAKER
Buck Baker, father of Buddy, earned 46 NASCAR victories and 44 pole positions, and was the first back-to-back champion of NASCAR's top series following the 1956 and 1957 seasons.

BUDDY BAKER
Buddy stepped out of the shadow of his father Buck with a long and successful NASCAR career. Baker won 19 races including the 1980 Daytona 500 and back-to-back Coca-Cola 600s in 1972 and 1973.

GEOFFREY BODINE
The 1982 Raybestos Rookie of the Year and winner of the 1986 Daytona 500, Bodine became an owner-driver when he purchased a team that began racing in 1993.

Buddy Baker

NEIL BONNETT
Bonnett won 18 races during his 17-year driving career, including back-to-back victories in 1982 and 1983 in NASCAR's longest race, the Coca-Cola 600, held in North Carolina.

ROBERT "RED" BYRON
Although Byron only competed in three NASCAR seasons, he was the winner of the first NASCAR-sanctioned race in 1948. The next year, he became the first overall NASCAR season champion.

JERRY COOK
After winning six NASCAR Whelen Modified Tour titles from 1971 to 1977, Cook became a key NASCAR official.

DALE EARNHARDT
Perhaps the most talented driver in the history of NASCAR, Dale Earnhardt won seven season championships, the last in 1994. Earnhardt's hard-driving style earned him 76 race wins, placing him sixth on the all-time wins list.

RALPH EARNHARDT
After dominating short tracks in North Carolina, Ralph won NASCAR's Sportsman Division championship in 1956 and raced in NASCAR NEXTEL Cup races from 1956 to 1964.

BILL ELLIOTT
"Awesome Bill from Dawsonville" was the NASCAR champion in 1988, and has won 44 races on NASCAR's top circuit. Elliott was voted Most Popular Driver a record 16 times.

RICHIE EVANS
The unquestioned king of modified racing, Evans won nine NASCAR Whelen Modified Tour championships between 1973 and 1985.

CHARLES "RED" FARMER
Farmer won three consecutive NASCAR Grand National Division championships from 1969 to 1971. He won numerous track championships in his adopted state of Alabama and competed well into his 70s.

TIM FLOCK
Flock, a member of the racing Flock family, was the NASCAR champion in 1952 and 1955. He won 40 races and 37 pole positions in 13 years behind the wheel. His 21.2 percent winning percentage (40 victories in 189 starts) is the best in the history of NASCAR's top Series.

Bill Elliott

A.J. FOYT
Better known for his four victories in the Indianapolis 500, Foyt was also a success in stock-car racing, winning seven NASCAR races, including the 1972 Daytona 500. Foyt has recieved many honors and awards over his professional driving career, including being co-named Best Driver of the Century (with Mario Andretti) by the Associated Press. Foyt is the father of NASCAR driver Larry Foyt.

HARRY GANT
In September 1991, Gant won a record-tying four consecutive NASCAR races. He also won two NASCAR Grand National Division races during that time.

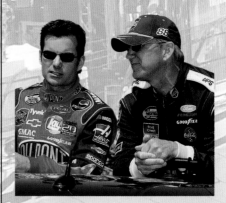

Jeff Gordon and Dale Jarrett

JEFF GORDON
Gordon has won four NASCAR championships (1995, 1997, 1998, and 2001) and 70 races. His major victories include the 1997, 1999, and 2005 Daytona 500s, the inaugural Brickyard 400 at Indianapolis Motor Speedway in 1994 and 1998, and four consecutive Southern 500s at Darlington Raceway from 1995 to 1998.

RAY HENDRICK
Hendrick's racing career spans 34 years, most of which were spent competing in NASCAR Modifieds. Some records indicate that Ray won more than 712 races.

JACK INGRAM
Ingram had great success in the NASCAR Grand National Division. He won three straight championships from 1972 to 1974, a fourth in 1982, and a fifth in 1985. His quintet of second-series championships is an all-time record.

ERNIE IRVAN
The winner of the 1991 Daytona 500, Irvan finished a career-best fifth in the series points race. After a bad accident in 1995, Irvan struggled back from his injuries and returned to the cockpit just 37 races later, finishing sixth in the October race at the North Wilkesboro Speedway.

BOBBY ISAAC
Through a 15-year career, Bobby Isaac won 37 NASCAR NEXTEL Cup Series races, which ranks him 16th on the all-time wins list. In 1970, he was the champion of NASCAR's top series.

DALE JARRETT

A two-time Daytona 500 winner, Jarrett's most successful season came in 1999, when he won the season championship, four races, and scored 29 top-10 finishes.

NED JARRETT

"Gentleman Ned" was the NASCAR champion in 1961 and 1965 and the winner of 50 NASCAR NEXTEL Cup Series races. He also won the championship in the series below the NNCS. His son Dale became a top racer.

JUNIOR JOHNSON

Johnson's aggressive driving style earned him 50 NASCAR wins, tying him with Ned Jarrett for 10th on the all-time win list. Johnson also found success as a car owner, winning 119 races and six championships.

ALAN KULWICKI

As an owner-driver, Kulwicki claimed the 1992 season championship.

TERRY LABONTE

Terry Labonte won the NASCAR championship in 1984 and again 12 years later in 1996. He had 21 race wins during his 655 consecutive NASCAR starts, a streak that ended in 2000. Terry and his brother Bobby are the only brothers to both win titles on NASCAR's highest level.

FRED LORENZEN

An example of Lorenzen's driving skills came in 1964 when he won eight of the 16 races he entered. In 1963, he was the first driver in NASCAR history to earn more than $100,000 in one season.

DEWAYNE "TINY" LUND

Lund was a very large for a driver, so his nickname was ironic. He won two NASCAR NEXTEL Cup races in a 21-year career. In February 1963, Lund rescued fellow driver Marvin Panch from a burning car during a practice session at Daytona.

MARK MARTIN

Martin has finished as the NASCAR runner-up on four occasions. Martin is also the career victories leader in the series below the NNCS, with 47 wins.

HERSCHEL MCGRIFF

McGriff's racing career spanned six decades of NASCAR competition—winning at least once in every decade from the 1950s to the 1990s.

Mark Martin

EVERETT "COTTON" OWENS

Owens won more than 200 NASCAR Whelen Modified Tour races during the 1950s before making the transition to the top NASCAR racing series. For six straight years (1957–1962), Owens won at least one race, finishing second overall in 1959.

MARVIN PANCH

The winner of 17 NASCAR NEXTEL Cup races, Panch had one of his most memorable wins came in the 1961 Daytona 500.

BENNY PARSONS

The 1973 NASCAR champion, Parsons earned 21 race wins. Two of his biggest came at the 1975 Daytona 500 and the 1980 Coca-Cola 600.

DAVID PEARSON

Pearson, a three-time NASCAR NEXTEL Cup champion, is second on NASCAR NEXTEL Cup's all-time win list with 105 wins, second only to Richard Petty.

LEE PETTY

Petty's 54 wins were a NASCAR record when he retired in 1964. They're still good enough to make him the ninth-best of all-time. In 1954, Lee won the first of three NASCAR overall championships, following up with titles in 1958 and 1959 to become the first three-time overall champion. He was also the winner of the first Daytona 500 in 1959.

RICHARD PETTY

The undisputed "King of Stock Car Racing" with 200 NASCAR NEXTEL Cup Series wins, Petty won seven series championships during his 35-year career. In the most remarkable season in NASCAR history, he won 27 of 48 races, including a record 10 straight, and finished second 7 times in cruising to the 1967 title.

TIM RICHMOND

In 1986, Richmond won seven races, more than any other driver, and finished a career-high third in the NASCAR NEXTEL Cup points race. He started in just eight races in 1987, winning two victories, one pole position, and tallying three top-five and four top-10 finishes.

GLEN "FIREBALL" ROBERTS

Perhaps the greatest driver never to win a NASCAR NEXTEL Cup title, Roberts accumulated 32 wins, including the 1962 Daytona 500, in a career that spanned 15 seasons.

RICKY RUDD

Rudd won Raybestos Rookie of the Year honors in 1977 and later went onto a remarkable 16-year streak of winning at least one race every season through 1998. He eventually became a car owner-driver.

MARSHALL TEAGUE

Teague enjoyed his best season in 1951, winning five of his career seven NASCAR wins in the top series.

HERB THOMAS

Thomas was NASCAR champion in 1951 and 1953. He won 48 races in 230 starts.

CURTIS TURNER

Turner was a vital part of early NASCAR stock car racing, leading in laps led, laps completed, and races led in 1950.

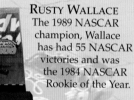

RUSTY WALLACE

The 1989 NASCAR champion, Wallace has had 55 NASCAR victories and was the 1984 NASCAR Rookie of the Year.

Rusty Wallace

DARRELL WALTRIP

A three-time champion (1981, 1982, and 1985) in NASCAR's top series, Darrell's 809 starts are fifth-best and his 84 victories ties him for third (with Bobby Allison) on the all-time list.

JOE WEATHERLY

Weatherly won back-to-back NASCAR championships in 1962 and 1963.

BOB WELBORN

From 1955 to 1957, Welborn won the final three NASCAR Convertible championships.

REX WHITE

The 1960 NASCAR champion, White finished in the top-10 in the point standings six of the nine years he competed on NASCAR's elite circuit.

GLEN WOOD

After a successful driving career, Glen and his brother Leonard formed one of the most successful racing teams in NASCAR history, winning 97 races.

CALE YARBOROUGH

The only NASCAR driver to win three straight championships (from 1976 to 1978), Cale Yarborough earned 83 NASCAR victories and 70 pole positions in a career that spanned four decades. He was also a four-time winner of the Daytona 500.

LEEROY YARBROUGH

Yarbrough's best season was in 1969 when he won seven races and racked up 21 top-10 finishes.

Find out more

THE BEST WAY TO EXPERIENCE the thrill of NASCAR is to go to a race, of course, but not everyone can go to a race every year. However, there are still plenty of ways for racing fans to enjoy NASCAR excitement year-round. From local short-track races to visits to museums to tours of famous tracks, fans can get up close and personal with NASCAR. More and more media outlets are increasing their NASCAR coverage, offering movies, TV shows, and more to help fans stay on top of the action. These pages show you just a few ways you can live the NASCAR life!

Cars lined up on Broadway in New York City

A fast-moving camera truck was used to track the action using large IMAX cameras.

YEAR-END CELEBRATION
NASCAR cars are shown here are on a "victory lap" around midtown Manhattan, starting in legendary Times Square, before the annual year-end NASCAR awards banquet. At the event, which is televised nationwide, top drivers and teams receive their final awards and winnings.

NASCAR AT THE MOVIES
This photo shows a special rolling IMAX camera, strapped to a pickup truck, getting up-close film of NASCAR action. The film, captured in shoots like this one, was used to create the visuallly dazzling IMAX movie NASCAR 3D.

This car is racing in one of eight regional series

TRACKS GALORE
You don't have to be located near a top NASCAR NEXTEL Cup track to see great racing. This car is racing in a Dodge Weekly event, one of the many local races across the nation.

USEFUL WEB SITES

www.nascar.com
NASCAR's official Web site, for everything you need to know about the sport. Fans can now also join the the NASCAR Members Club by clicking on the link on www.nascar.com.

www.nascarcafe.com
Find the locations of NASCAR Cafes near you, where you can see collections of NASCAR-themed memorabilia, buy sportswear and souvenirs, and enjoy delicious food.

www.nascarspeedparks.com
Check out the locations and features of these super-fast NASCAR-themed amusement parks.

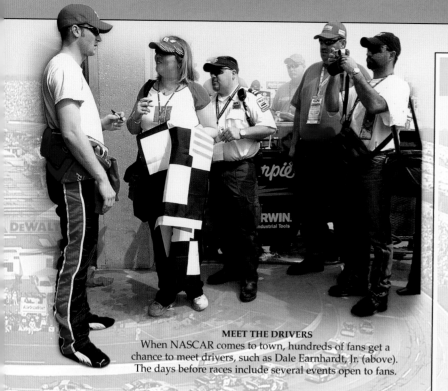

MEET THE DRIVERS
When NASCAR comes to town, hundreds of fans get a chance to meet drivers, such as Dale Earnhardt, Jr. (above). The days before races include several events open to fans.

Other racing series

While most fans are aware of the three national series in NASCAR, other stock-car racing series, held at smaller tracks around the country, are less well-known, but just as exciting.

NASCAR WEST SERIES

MORE WAYS TO RACE
NASCAR West is one of eight regional series that make up the Dodge Weekly Series.

NASCAR WHELEN MODIFIED TOUR

UNIQUE LOOK
Cars on the Whelen Modified Tour (see picture below) are the most unusual looking types of cars in the NASCAR family.

NASCAR DODGE WEEKLY SERIES

NASCAR AutoZone ELITE DIVISION

MOVING UP
Following NASCAR's three national series, the AutoZone Elite Division races feature excellent drivers.

REGIONAL RACING
On dirt and asphalt tracks in four divisions around the country, drivers compete in smaller stock cars for regional and national honors in this series.

WILD DESIGN
One type of racing in the NASCAR Regional Series is done in modified cars such as this one. Stripped-down stock cars, they usually race on very short tracks with tight turns.

Places and events

NASCAR PRESEASON THUNDER
Every January, fans flock to Daytona International Speedway for NASCAR Preseason Thunder—a series of preseason test sessions for the drivers. This exciting annual spectacle takes place January 11–24.

NASCAR CAFE
Fans looking for a tasty connection to their favorite motor sport can pay a visit to a NASCAR Cafe. Each of these NASCAR-themed restaurants includes collections of memorabilia from car parts to driver gear. A store inside each cafe lets fans pick up the latest souvenirs and sportswear featuring their favorite drivers. And the menu is full of food that families enjoy. NASCAR Cafes are located in Las Vegas; Myrtle Beach, South Carolina; Orlando, Florida; Greensboro, North Carolina; Johnson City, Tennessee; and Smoky Mountain, Tennessee.

NASCAR SPEED PARKS
These unique amusement parks combine the thrill of racing with tons of fun for the whole family. Tracks and cars for all ages are available, along with a high-tech arcade. Miniature golf, bumper boats, and a store featuring NASCAR gear round out the NASCAR Speed Park experience. NASCAR Speed Parks can be found in Myrtle Beach, South Carolina; Concord, North Carolina; St. Louis, Missouri; Toronto, Ontario; and Sevierville, Tennessee.

ALL-AMERICAN SOAP BOX DERBY
NASCAR now helps support this 70-year-old "kit racing" program, the premier youth and family racing activity in the United States. At races around the country, kids from 8 to 17 race in small, gravity-powered cars that they have made themselves from kits. They're all aiming for the finals, held each July in Akron, Ohio.

A VISIT TO DAYTONA USA
This museum complex is located in Daytona Beach, Florida, alongside the most famous track in NASCAR. Fans can visit the exciting hands-on interactive attractions at the museum, find memorabilia at the gift shop, take tours of the facilities, and even, at certain times, take a lap around the track itself. At the museum entrance (above) a fan shoots a photo of a statue of Dale Earnhardt, the 1998 Daytona 500 champ.

Glossary

AERODYNAMICS In racing, the study of how air flows over, under, and around a moving car

AIR DAM A metal strip that hangs beneath the front grill, often just inches from the ground; helps provide aerodynamic downforce at the front of the car.

AIR PRESSURE Force exerted by air that keeps a tire inflated; measured in pounds per square inch (psi)

Air dam

APRON The paved portion of a racetrack that separates the racing surface, where cars drive, from the infield

BANKING The sloping of a racetrack, particularly at a curve or corner, from the apron to the outside wall. The degree of banking, when given as a number, refers to the angle of the track surface.

BLISTER If tire tread overheats, bubbles known as blisters can appear on the surface.

BLOWN MOTOR Major engine failure during a race; usually produces a lot of smoke and steam and will often knock a driver and his car out of a race

BODYWORK The fabricated sheet metal that encloses the chassis

CAMSHAFT A rotating shaft within the engine that opens and closes the valves in the engine

CARBURETOR A device connected directly to the gas pedal and mounted on top of the engine that controls the mixture of fuel and air fed to the pistons

CHASSIS The steel structure or frame of the car

CHUTE The straight part of a racetrack, also called a straightaway

CONTACT PATCH The portion of the tire that makes contact with the racing surface. The size of each tire's contact patch changes as the car is driven. The patch on the tires closest to the inside of a track might be larger than those on the outside.

CRANKSHAFT The rotating shaft within the engine that delivers the power from the pistons through the engine to the transmission and the wheels (see p. 22)

CUT TIRE A slice or puncture of the tread or sidewall of a tire, often caused by debris on the track or by a collision with some part of another car

CYLINDER HEAD One of two pieces of aluminum, bolted to the top of each side of the engine block, that hold the valves and spark plugs. Passages through the cylinder heads make up the intake and exhaust ports.

DECK LID Slang term for the trunk lid of a NASCAR race car

DIRTY AIR Turbulent air currents caused by fast moving cars that can cause a car to lose control

DONUTS Slang term for black, circular marks on the side panels of stock cars, usually caused by rubbing against other cars at high speed. Also, slang term for the dirt-churning circles turned on the infield by celebrating victorious drivers.

DOWNFORCE The force that helps hold a fast-moving car to the track. The more downforce, the more grip the car has. The design of the car combines with the speed to create downforce.

DRAFT Slang term for the aerodynamic effect that allows two or more cars that are traveling nose-to-tail to run faster than a single car. When one car follows another closely, the one in front cuts through the air, creating less resistance for the car in back.

DRAFTING The practice of two or more cars running nose-to-tail, almost touching, during a race. The lead car, by cutting through the air in front of it, creates a vacuum between its rear end and the nose of the following car, thus pulling the second car along with it.

DRAG The resistance a car experiences when passing through air at high speeds

ENGINE BLOCK An iron casting that forms the basic shape of the engine

FABRICATOR A person who specializes in creating the sheet metal body of a stock car. Most teams employ two or more.

FIREWALL A solid metal plate that separates the engine compartment from the driver's compartment of the race car

FLAT-OUT Slang term for racing a car as fast as possible under the given weather and track conditions

FRAME The interior metal structure of a racecar, on which the sheet metal of the car's body is shaped. Also called a *chassis*.

FUEL The gasoline that powers the engine of the car

FUEL CELL A holding tank for a race car's gasoline; a product of aerospace technology, designed to eliminate or minimize fuel spillage

GAUGE An instrument, usually mounted on the dashboard, used to monitor engine conditions such as fuel pressure, oil pressure, water pressure, temperature, and RPM (revolutions per minute)

GROOVE Slang term for the best route around the racetrack; the most efficient or quickest way around the track for a particular driver. The "high groove" takes a car closer to the outside wall of the track for most of a lap, while the "low groove" takes a car closer to the apron than the outside wall. Road racers use the term "line" to describe the various grooves on a track. Drivers always search for a fast groove, but the location of such grooves often changes depending on the weather and the condition of the track.

A pair of cars on a high groove

HANDLING A racecar's performance while racing, qualifying, and practicing. How a car handles is determined by its design, aerodynamics, tire pressure, and other factors.

HAULER The 18-wheel tractor-trailer rig that teams use to transport race cars, engines, tools, and support equipment to the racetracks. Cars are stowed in the top section, while the bottom floor is used for work space.

IGNITION An electrical system used to ignite the air-fuel mixture in an internal combustion engine; starts the car's engine for a race.

LAPPED TRAFFIC Cars that have completed at least one full lap less than the race leader

LEAD LAP The lap that the race leader is currently on

LUG NUTS Large nuts applied with a high-pressure air wrench to the wheel during a pit stop to secure the tires in place. All NASCAR cars use five lug nuts on each wheel.

MARBLES Excess rubber build-up above the upper groove on the racetrack; also known as "loose stuff"

Lug nuts

PISTON A circular part that moves up and down in the cylinder in the engine

PIT ROAD The area where pit crews service the cars; generally located along the front straightaway. Because of space limitations, some racetracks sport pit roads on both the front and back straightaways.

POLE POSITION Slang term for the best position on the starting grid, awarded to the fastest qualifier; located on the inside of the front row of the starting grid of 43 cars

QUARTER-PANEL Pieces of sheet metal making up part of the sides of a car

RESTART The waving of the green flag following a caution period

RESTRICTOR PLATE A thin metal plate with four holes that restricts airflow from the carburetor into the engine; used to reduce horsepower and keep speeds down at some superspeedways

Two drivers as they start a NASCAR race

ROLL CAGE The steel tubing inside the race car's interior. Designed to protect the driver from impacts or rollovers, roll cages must meet strict NASCAR safety guidelines and are inspected regularly.

SLINGSHOT A maneuver in which a car following the leader in a draft suddenly pulls around it; provides an extra burst of speed that allows the second car to take the lead

SPOILER A metal blade attached to the rear deck lid of the car; helps restrict airflow over the rear of the car, providing downforce and traction

TEMPLATE A device used to check the car's body shape and size, to ensure compliance with the rules; closely resembles the shape of the factory version of the car

TRADING PAINT Slang term used to describe aggressive driving involving a lot of bumping and rubbing

TRI-OVAL A race track with a "hump" or fifth turn in addition to the standard four turns or corners; not to be confused with a triangle-shaped speedway with three corners, a configuration not currently used in any NASCAR races

VICTORY LANE The spot on each racetrack's infield where the race winner parks for the celebration; sometimes called the "winner's circle"

WEDGE Small adjustments to the weight or distribution of weight on the car can greatly affect the handling of the car. Racing team members use small weights called "wedges" to make these adjustments before or even during a race.

WIND TUNNEL A structure used by race teams to determine the aerodynamic efficiency of their vehicles, consisting of a platform on which the vehicle is fixed and a giant fan which creates an enormous wind that flows over the body of the car while measurements are taken of the air flow

WINDOW NET A woven mesh that hangs across the car driver's side window

Using a template

Index

Acknowledgments

From the author/producer: Just as a NASCAR driver can't capture the checkered flag without a top-notch crew, so, too, this book would not have happened without a great team of pros. Beth Hester at DK was our crew chief and she ran the job like a pro. Thanks to designer Diana Catherines and editor Laura Buller for going "over the wall" so well. Thanks to Tai Blanche for hanging in there when every second counted. Catherine McNeill at NASCAR Publishing was our fantastic team "owner," making sure everything ran just the right way. Thanks to photographers George Tiedemann, Scott Hunter, and Dave Mager for their fine work. Sherryl Creekmore's eye and access helped give us some great behind-the-scenes photos. Our team had a great time making this book . . .we hope you think it's a winner.

PHOTOGRAPHY CREDITS
(t: top, b: bottom, r: right, l: left, c: center)

AP/Wide World: 10tl, tr, b, 11tr, 13br; 14cl, br; 15t, cr, br, bl; 16tl; 17tl, tc; 21cr; 22tl; 26tl, cr, bc; 29tl, tc, tr; 32tl; 35tl (2); 37tl; 38bl; 39br; 44tl; 45tl; 45tl, bl, br; 47bl, br, cr; 48tr; 49tr; 52tl, cl, b; 53tr` 55br; 57b; 58c, b; 59cl, bl; 64bl; 69bl, br; 71bc. Brian Bahr/Getty Images: 52tr. Jim Cooper/Getty Images: 16bl. CIA Stock Photos: 31l. Corbis/Bettmann: 11tl, cr, br; 12cr; 13cr; 14tr; 30tc; 34tl; 38tl; 44bl; 45cr (medal); 59tl; 62tr. Corbis: 17tr; 32tr; 64-65 bkgd.; 70-71 bkgd. DK Picture Library: 25t, bl, cr. Jonathan Ferrey/Getty Images: 25br; 27c; 46b; 61b. Scott Gries/Getty Images: 18cr. Charlene Ingham/Getty Images: 68c. Rusty Jarrett/Getty Images: 6tr, bl; 23tr; 24tl; 43tc; 62c; 63tr. Michael Kim/Getty Images: 39tl. Robert

Laberge/Getty Images: 6br; 19tl; 64t. Gavin Lawrence/Getty Images: 71tr. David Mager for DK (objects from author's collection): 8tr, bc; 12tr (2); 14tl, c; 16br; 18tl; 39tr (3); 44b (model); 45cr (box); 46tr; 47t (5); 48tl (3); 53b (bottle); 54tl; 56tr; 57cr (hat); 58tl, tr, bl; 59tr. Al Messerschmidt/Sports Gallery: 18tr, bc; 27tr; 35b; 42tl; 54c; 55tr; 60cl (2), tr, cr; 61tr. Frank Micelotta/Getty Images: 19tr. Gilles Mingason/Getty Images: 38cr. Donald Miralle/Getty Images: 6cl; NASCAR: diagrams on 20bl; 25tr; 26tr; 33tr (4); photos: 46tl; 61tl, c; 62tl; 68bl, tr. NASCAR/Sherryl Creekmore: 6tl, 7tr, bl; 21b; 28tl, c, b; 32bl; 40bl, tr; 41tl, tr, b; 43tr; 45tr; 48br; 49tc, bc, b; 50 (5); 51tl, b, cr; 53cr, br; 54cl, bl, b; 55tl, cr; 56cl, cr; 57tr; 59br; 63tl; 64br; 69tl; 70br. NASCAR/Al: 58tl, 9tl, 12b; 20tl, 44lc, bc. Courtesy NBC Sports: 60bl. Nightwings/Scott Hunter: 21tl; 22-23 (7); 24cl (7), tc; 25bl; 26bl;

27tl (2); 34bl (6); 37tr (3); 43tc; 54tr; 62l, b (5); 71cl. Bob Peterson/Getty Images: 44c. Mike Powell/Getty Images: 16tr. Joe Robbins: 16cr; 17br; 26cl; 27b; 33b; 35tr; 36b, tr; 37cl, bl; 38br; 49cl. Courtesy Simpson Racing Products: 21tc; 30cl; 31r (5); 42tl, bl, cr, cl. Courtesy Sports Immortals: 13tl; 30br. Jamie Squire/Getty Images: 56bl; 57tl; 63b. Chris Stanford/Getty Images: 51tl. Allen Steele/Getty Images: 44br. David Taylor/Getty Images: 29bc; 48bl; 56tl. George Tiedemann: 8cr, cl; 9b; 13tr; 14bl; 29tc; 30tl (2); 38tr; 40tl; 46cl. Todd Warshaw/Getty Images: 18bl; 65tl.

Jacket credits:
Front: George Tiedemann: tl. Simpon Racing Products: tcl, bcl. Sherryl Creekmore/NASCAR: tr. Corbis: tr. NASCAR: b. Back: George Tiedemann: cr. Dave Mager: tl, tr, cl. AP Photo/Chris Gardner: b.